POSITIVELY INFLUENTIAL

Top Professional Networking and Attraction Marketing Secrets from the Real World

**VOLUME 1
(EPISODES 1-10)**

by

Rob Christensen

**50™
Interviews**

www.50networkers.com

Positively Influential: Top Professional Networking and Attraction Marketing Secrets from the Real World (Vol. 1)
Copyright © 2010 by Rob Christensen
http://attractionmarketing.50interviews.com

ISBN 978-1-935689-11-9

Published by Wise Media Group
444 17th Street, Suite 507
Denver, CO 80202
http://www.WiseMediaGroup.com

Original *50 Interviews* concept by Brian Schwartz
Cover by Nick Zelinger of NZ Graphics
Interior layout by Veronica Yager of YellowStudios
First edition. Printed in the United States of America.

To my father "Big Bob" Christensen,
Pioneer of the New South Wales cotton industry,
freelance irrigation engineer and storyteller.

I once found myself in a pub in Nyngan, N.S.W. with a group of fellow classmates and professors from the Geology faculty of the University of Sydney. I don't remember the exact conversation, but it resulted in a bet that someone in the bar, if they had anything to do with cotton, would know my dad. The first person I asked said;

"Big Bob Christensen?
That bloke could make water run uphill!"

I didn't realize it at the time,
but this was your professional networking.

You taught me the value of going above and beyond for your clients. Of making sure that the job was done well, and in time for the farmers to get their crops in, so that they could make a profit too.

You also gave me a love for stories, and storytelling. I am reminded at family gatherings that we are not alone in this, and it seems to be a family trait.

Thanks Dad!

Bob Christensen
1928 - 2010

ACKNOWLEDGEMENTS

I would like to thank and express my sincere appreciation to all the individuals who helped and supported me in my work to complete this book: Positively Influential: Top Professional Networking and Attraction Marketing Secrets from the Real World, amid so many other projects and a crazy work schedule.

To Brian Schwartz, my publisher, mentor and friend. I met Brian in a professional networking context. We were part of a small business peer advisory board together. Brian provided value to others and received value from others, without pushing his own agenda. He once asked "What would you do if someone offered you a million dollars for your business?" I lightly responded "Sell it and start a new business, with no debt and cash reserves!" Brian then told me I was probably in the wrong business. He was right. Thank you Brian, for your encouragement, ideas and support, as well as the infrastructure you have built to help aspiring new authors. As a result, when the time was right, it was a joy to be able to work with you on this project.

To Dave Block, who is Co-Founder of the "Make-It-Fly" small business advisory board, where I met Brian Schwartz. I learned so much from you and all the others on our Make-It-Fly board. Although I never launched the business that I was planning and building at the time, the people I met through Make-It-Fly, the relationships that were started, and the things that I learned, made it an invaluable experience and indirectly resulted in the creation of this book. Dave, you are one of the great "connectors" and a true networking professional.

To Sandi Gardner-Wood, Founder of "Divinely Clean," The dear friend who listened with enthusiasm to my entrepreneurial dream (while cleaning my house), and told me "If you are really going to do this, You have to give Dave Block a call!" Sandi's husband Joseph Wood was Best Man at my wedding.

You see how this "networking thing" works...

I would also like to thank my dear wife Angela, for putting up with me hiding away in my office for hours at a time, for proof reading some of my work, and for being a pleasant distraction from working on my book from time-to-time as well.

To my friend Karl Busch, for patiently listening to my verbal processing of new attraction marketing ideas, and for being a sounding board.

To all of my interviewees, for taking the time to answer my questions and openly sharing your unique insights gained from real-world experience. Without you, this book would not have been possible. Your real-world experience bridges the gap between theory and practice.

The importance of this real-world experience is best said in a quote that has been attributed to several different people from Yogi Berra, to Albert Einstein, to Jan L.A. van de Snepscheut: "In theory, there is no difference between theory and practice. But, in practice, there is!"

TABLE OF CONTENTS

INTRODUCTION

Have you ever been to a party, or some type of business networking event, where someone you barely know, or don't know at all, latches on to you and starts telling you all about their business in mind-numbing detail?

They start trying to sell you insurance, or whatever their deal is... "OK, so you have insurance, but you could always use a little more. Am I right? Or am I right? Right? Right?" You feel like Phil Connors in Groundhog Day, being assailed by "Needle Nose" Ned Ryerson. What is the typical response of people caught in that situation? Is it polite endurance? Finding an excuse to be somewhere else? Feigning a seizure, or even death, to get them to leave you alone?

This approach may be influential, but few would call it a positive influence. One thing is for sure. You don't like it when people do this to you, and you certainly don't ever want to be "That Guy!" It is just not very attractive. The guy brings no value whatsoever to you – or at least fails to communicate any real value.

That is the key. Mr Ryerson may actually have the best insurance policy with the best value in the marketplace. It may even be better than yours, and save you a couple of hundred dollars a year. But because of his unprofessional networking and marketing style; you will never know, or care.

Yet billions of dollars worth of business is transacted over lunch, or at the golf course. People get referrals from their friends and business associates all the time; and they give them. Word of mouth is said to be the best form of advertising.

Successful business people network with other successful business people. They carefully cultivate real relationships and build a network with people who have skill sets and resources that they themselves may not have. They trust each other to take care of their clients and customers if they give a referral, and they take care of people who are referred to them.

A good referral is more than just a name and a phone number. It is somebody who knows who you are when you call them, and says something like "Oh Rob! Thank you so much for calling..." or "I've been expecting your call! Joe said that you could help me out with..."

Wouldn't you like to hear more of that when you call someone about your business?

This is a lot better than cold calling someone who doesn't have the faintest idea of who you are, or why on earth they should give you five minutes of their time to find out.

And it isn't just for salespeople or entrepreneurs. People who are looking for work also find jobs through networking. Through people they know. Or people, that know people they know. A lot of jobs aren't even advertised in traditional media. If you wait until you are laid off before starting to build your network, it can take a long time to develop relationships that might help your resume get noticed.

But networking isn't all about just what you can get out of other people. Attractive networking; professional networking, is also about what you can give. Influence isn't always about getting others to do what you want. It is also about helping and empowering people to reach their own goals.

Whether you are a "floor guy" or a politician, a teacher, coach or consultant, employee or entrepreneur; if you are in direct sales or service, whatever you do, your business is people. They are the lifeblood of your business. Ignore them at your peril. Take advantage of them and you will earn their distrust. Abusing people is not only a poor business model, it is also most unattractive.

"All other things being equal,
people do business with those,
they know, like and trust."

I generally, genuinely like people. I like meeting new people, and often end up enjoying a conversation with someone, who a few moments before was a complete stranger. Sometimes this drives my wife nuts! So why was it so hard to transition from my personal networking skills to professional networking skills when I started marketing for a direct sales company to produce a part-time income?

Many direct sales companies want new people to make a list of 100 friends, family, and neighbors; so they can share their brand new business with them. This works for some people. Others have a problem even getting started. They barely know what they are doing, and with nervousness and enthusiasm, sometimes come off a little like "Needle Nose" Ned.

I still had plenty of great conversations. I just had a very hard time closing sales. It did not seem to flow naturally, and I couldn't seem to find people who wanted my product enough to part with their hard earned cash. A friend of mine told me that this is all a matter of perceived value. When the product's value to somebody exceeds the value of the money they would have to spend to get it; then a transaction can take place, but not before. But how do you communicate value, and how do you get people to listen?

There had to be a better way to do business! People buy things all the time. They like to buy things! People generally just don't like being manipulated and sold. So how do you find people who want what you have to offer, and communicate value to them without alienating them? This is the million dollar question! What would you be willing to do to find the answer?

After talking with my friend Brian Schwartz, Author of 50 Interviews: Entrepreneurs, I decided to start interviewing people with real-world experience. People who have learned how to network in a professional manner; not chasing after friends and acquaintances – or those who have no interest in what they have to offer, and instead attract people who are interested in finding out more.

This is called attraction marketing. It should not be confused with the popularized "law of attraction", although some attraction marketers do believe in and use the latter. They are two different things.

If you are interested in learning from people who have achieved real-world success in professional networking and attraction marketing, and if you have good intentions of providing real value to people whether or not they become your customers and clients, taking care of them, helping them to achieve their goals, and not just trying to manipulate them to your own ends, then this book is for you.

It will help you cultivate relationships upon which trust can be built, and create an environment where sales and referrals can take place, if there is a need for your product or service.

ONE

Networking not only grows your business, it's a great way to make friends!
Barbara Silva, Co-Founder of Coaching Cognition

Barbara Silva has managed to achieve her five year plan in two years!

A former career teacher, Barbara was confined to bed with illness for four and a half months. During this time she began to build an online presence which, over a couple of years, has lead to her writing a book, coaching coaches and co-founding a coaching platform with her mentor Mike Klingler.

Barbara grew up in Santa Barbara, California and obtained her BA in English and MA in English and education at Pepperdine University in Malibu. With a minor in drama, she also spent a little time in acting school in San Diego. Working very closely with her professors and other students in this small school in Malibu helped her with networking and her teaching career. Her first job out of college was teaching middle school English and Drama. She did this for several years, before becoming a research assistant and editor at the USC School of Medicine, where she did research for a book on how doctors learn and keep up with advances in their field. This research experience helped with her future work in coaching but the experience that helped her most in this arena was the years she spent working in a private pre-school program.

Working with very young children who didn't always have language abilities yet, Barbara had to learn how to put the puzzle pieces together, to figure out what the secret was to each child and how to reach that child. At the same time; she was working with new parents and helping them see the challenges they had as parents as something that is actually a positive step in the child's growth. For example; when a child starts becoming independent and starts resisting rules in the household, Barbara helped parents see that this is something that has to be managed, but it is a normal, healthy development in the child. Barbara wound up doing a lot of listening and understanding the other person's point of view in order to be able to communicate with them.

No matter what age Barbara wound up working with, she learned from her students constantly; from two year-olds to Introduction to Literature college students.

Her ability to learn from her students and from other teachers helped her with networking and in her later career in coaching. With Barbara's varied teaching experiences as a foundation for launching her own business, she is the author of Romancing the Sale and co-founder of CoachingCognition.com, along with her mentor, Mike Klingler.

Q. Is being able to learn from the other people that you are working with, and not just try to sell them stuff, a big part of networking?

A. Yes, exactly! It's getting to know people and being able to communicate with them so that both of you come away having benefitted from the exchange. That involves being truly interested in the other person whether or not you think there is something that they can do for you. It has to be born out of really being interested in what other people are doing, why they are doing it, what their dreams are, what's working for them, what isn't. You learn along the way as you do that, even if it's in a field completely outside of your own.

Q. Was there anything in your early life that you learned from, that later helped you with networking, interpersonal relationships or with attraction marketing?

A. I had a French class and there was no teacher for the class at the beginning of the year. The substitute teacher actually didn't speak French and I did, so in the first couple of weeks of school, the substitute teacher would turn the class over to me because I at least knew a little bit and could lead the class. So when they hired the new teacher, I guess she felt a little uncomfortable that I might think I was going to be continuing to run the class as opposed to taking my role as a student. Her attitude toward me was not what I was used to. Usually I had really good relationships with my teachers and she didn't seem to like me very much.

I understood what the reason was. It is important to be able to put yourself in that other person's shoes and be able to look at things from the way they look at it. So I thought to myself, "What would it be like if she really did like me? What is it that she needs from me?" What she needed from me is to know that I wasn't going to be a problem and I wasn't going to try to continue in a role that I was not the least bit prepared for anyway. So I acted as if she liked me. I would find something in the lesson that had been particularly interesting. I would make a point of going up after class, sharing it with her, and saying, "You know: I really enjoyed this part of what you taught us today. Thank you so much for that." It was never something that wasn't true. Then I would leave. I didn't want to take up a bunch of her time because I knew that would be a problem too. I smiled at her. I made eye contact with her. I just acted as if she liked me. Over a period of maybe two or three weeks it completely changed the way she thought of me. Sure enough – she would wind up putting me in charge of certain things in the class, which was not particularly my goal; but we actually became very close.

So the solution was in meeting her needs, it was figuring out: What is her problem? What does she need, and how can I provide that? For her, it was helping establish her role as being the teacher, and me being a facilitator of that rather than a hindrance.

Q. When did you first start to get involved in networking or attraction marketing?

A. It was back in 2007. I had decided to go into business on my own and I went online because I didn't know anything about doing this – I had no business background at all. I had been working with a company, but they didn't teach anything about marketing. So I took myself on the Internet to learn about marketing. When I found the attraction marketing model; not only was it the thing that made sense to me, but it also was much more in alignment with my value system and comfort level. It is a whole lot easier to talk with people who have requested to talk with you, and who want to hear what it is that you have to say, than it is to be trying to push something down someone's throat that they are not the least bit interested in. So it fit really well with me.

Q. I suppose you don't hear that loud phone hang up as often?

A. You almost never do. In fact you tend to hear, "Oh my gosh! I can't' believe you finally called! Oh, it's so great to talk to you!" It's just a much, much nicer way

COACHING COGNITION

to do business.

Q. How long were you involved in networking or attraction marketing before you actually started to see some tangible results for your business?

A. I was very fortunate in the sense that I was able to work at it full time. I actually was ill and in bed for four and a half months and I couldn't do anything else, so it had my full attention and I worked very, very hard. It took a couple of months to build a bit of content, but I would say about five weeks from the time I actually had some content up online, my blog started getting traffic. I was taking a class with Mike Klingler and he was aware and watching what the different students were doing. I was implementing the teaching, and I guess I was doing it fairly well because he sent out an email about my blog and that I was on the right track with it. That got people to the site and, once they were at the site, very soon after that I started getting emails and phone calls from people.

Q. Were there any significant milestones or turning points along the way?

A. Certainly the day that Mike Klingler became aware of my work was a milestone. Another milestone was when I had enough content up in enough places that just gave value. I wasn't trying to sell anything at that point. I was just teaching what I knew or teaching what I learned, as I learned it. When I had enough content online that people were able to find me, then there started to be comments left on my blog and there started to be more action. So another milestone was the first time I made it to page one of Google for a competitive term like "network marketing", "Internet marketing" or "home-based business" – those kinds of terms. Showing up on page one of Google was definitely a milestone.

When I was able to communicate and form relation-ships with people, through social networks, the next milestone was simply through talking with people on the Internet and sharing experiences with each other. I found a need out there that I didn't think had been addressed. That was when I got the idea for writing *Romancing the Sale*. Writing this book gave me the first product that was mine, as opposed to just promoting something someone else had done. That was a huge milestone.

Then the next one, a logical progression from *Romanc-ing the Sale*, was building customer relationships. This led to more and more people asking for my coaching help, which opened up another need; and it happened to be a need that Mike Klingler was also aware of. So as he and I had become closer as associates on the Internet; me as a student of his, he came to me and together we formed the *Coaching Cognition* program. That, of course, was the icing on the cake for me! That was where I wanted to go.

It happened a lot faster than I thought it would. I had a five year business plan and I had set the goal that somewhere around the five-year mark somebody like Mike Klingler, hopefully Mike Klingler himself, would seek me out as a business partner. I think it was around the 18-month mark when it happened. Now, of course it took a long time to develop *Coaching Cogni-tion* from that point, but the coming together and the partnership formed much faster than I thought.

Q. **What makes the difference between an attractive networker, a boring networker and an irritating net-worker?**

A. An irritating networker is someone who is absorbed

in what may genuinely to them be something really important but isn't necessarily important to the people they are talking to. So even unintentionally, they wind up spamming. You can spam somebody at a dinner party, as well as you can spam them on the Internet. So an irritating networker is a person who goes on and on about what they are doing without ever checking to see if it's something that the other person is interested in.

A boring networker is one who may have something of value, but they haven't made the connection with how it ties into the needs of the people they are talking to. So I may have a wonderful program that I am talking about, but if I am not showing you "what is in it for you", how it is going to help you with something you are struggling with, it's going to be boring because it doesn't apply to you. You may be able to listen to it for five minutes, but you are not going to want to read all of my newsletters and articles, or open all of my emails, because that connection isn't there.

An attractive networker is someone who has tapped in to what that need is; to what it is that other people are searching for, what they are hungry for. They begin without asking anything of

> *"You can spam somebody at a dinner party, as well as you can spam them on the Internet."*

them, begin addressing their needs, and do it in such a way that it is always up to the person on the other end to seek out more information if they want it. That, to me, is attractive!

They are networkers who treat that person with what I call the "OPW" (Only Person in the World) mental-

BARBARA SILVA

ity. Even though they may be writing to thousands of people, the person reading what they have written feels like they are the only person in the world. You show that you really care about these other people and you can't fake that. It's got to be real. There has to be a genuine desire to help the other person and that's attractive. If you are in it just for yourself, that comes through too.

If you don't treat people that way, you might not see it at first but you'll find out later, there's a deep drop. There's a disappointment factor that can actually do you a lot more harm than good in having put that person on your list. Once somebody is networking with you, you have to treat them like the important resource and connection that they are, and be very, very careful that you treat them with respect and don't abuse that relationship in any way.

Q. What kind of things have you done consciously to improve your networking skills?

A. I have improved them by doing networking. I spent several months, close to a year, without really getting anything significant monetarily. I made a little bit of money here and there, but my focus was on the networking. It was on developing relationships. I did things like write articles for other people's blogs because they asked me to. I saw that it would be a nice way for me to be in front of a different audience, but it was also a way of helping out another networker, in making their job easier. As I did that, I formed very strong relationships and some of those people have since then grown their businesses in the same way that I have. I wound up having some pretty powerful alliances out there that I had no way of knowing, at the time, were going to happen. So I learned by doing, and I learned by watching what was attractive to me and what wasn't. I also learned by actually studying attraction marketing.

Q. Do you have any particular recommended training resources, books, classes, anything like that which come to mind?

A. For "how to" information on attraction marketing, I recommend *The Renegade Professional* because, whether you are a technical person or a non-technical person, it gives you step-by-step instructions on how to physically put articles up on the net, where to put them, and also teaches you what kinds of things to write about. It gives you a lot of information about the principle of attraction and what it is. I also recommend *Romancing the Sale* because it is based on being an attractive marketer and finding out where to go to find customers, and how to build relationships so you don't jump the gun and do something that makes you unattractive. Then, I also recommend, whether you do it with our program *Coaching Cognition* or other programs, to seek out coaching. Get a coach that can work with you, help you generate ideas, brainstorm, and move yourself forward. A lot of times what stops people is a lack of confidence and it's hard to get started. They know what they want to do, but it's just really hard to take that first step. So if you get a really good coach that knows how to get out of you what it is that you do want, and what it is that you need to do to make that happen, you will get there faster.

> *"A lot of times what stops people is a lack of confidence and it's hard to get started. They know what they want to do, but it's just really hard to take that first step."*

BARBARA SILVA

Q. **As someone with a lot of coaching experience, who has actually taught a lot of coaches, if I were someone who had never done any coaching before, what should I look for in choosing a coach?**

A. One of the most important things is just the rapport between you and the coach. A lot of people, statistically, hire the first coach they come across. It is okay to shop around and make sure your coach is someone you click with. The second thing is to know what it is that you want. There's a difference between a coach and a consultant. You go to a consultant if you need somebody to show you how to do something. If there is basically one way to do it, you bring in an expert on that subject. But if you want a coach, the coach works with you and instead of putting information into you, the coach brings information out of you. They are there to help make sure that everything you are doing fits in with the big picture of what is right for you, what's comfortable for you, and what's the best way for you to go about building your business. What works for one person isn't necessarily going to work for another. So the coach is trained to really listen to what your needs are and then help you get that into action. You don't just sit around and talk about it; you actually start doing it. In that light, there are a lot of people that refer to themselves as coaches, but they are actually consultants. So make sure that you are finding someone who is a coach, meaning that they are going to be working with you on what it is that you want, as opposed to telling you what it is that you want, or how you should do something.

When we think of coaches, we tend to think of sports coaches who are very much in control and they do tell people; they tell the athlete "Do 50 pushups", "Do this exercise" or whatever. Whereas in this kind of coaching, it's finding out that maybe 50 pushups isn't what

10

this athlete needs. Maybe this athlete already has that upper body strength and wants to train to be a runner. Therefore, they need a different set of exercises. Maybe pushups will work too, but maybe they need something completely different.

In coaching, it's customizing to this particular client; what it is they want and what will work best for them. A lot of people don't understand that. In fact, they want their coach to tell them what to do. Often as they work together, they start realizing that more is achieved by letting their coach help them find out what is true for them, because then, they are working on something that they really want. So their energy, creativity, and confidence levels go way up, and they've got somebody who is keeping them in action. So let's say your goal is to write a book; a lot of people just talk about the book but they never sit down to write it. Your coach will guide you with action steps that get you writing and make your book a reality.

Q. Are there any particular mistakes people make that are unforgivable in networking?

A. Unforgiveable is a difficult word for me because I am a pretty forgiving person. But big mistakes, possibly career busting mistakes, would be to not respect what another person is doing in their business. So as you network, if you wind up cross-promoting with someone, or you joint venture (JV) with someone so that you are allowed to promote something that you've done to their list, you have to understand that their list is the lifeblood of their business. Your list is the lifeblood of your business. The people that have contacted you and want to hear from you – this is the most important asset your business has. So one of the worst things you can do, would be to abuse the list – either yours or someone else's, by sending them junk; by rec-

Barbara Silva

ommending something that really is sub-standard but that you can make money from through an affiliate program. Your list deserves the best of what you have to offer at all times. If you are working with someone else's list, you are ethically bound to treat their list the same way as you would yours.

I also find a lot of people who are afraid of giving credit to other people; or recommending other trainers, other programs, other authors – this is a mistake as well. It is not necessarily a business-killing mistake, but it won't propel you forward. You can't be seen as a selfish marketer. If you see a program that's being done by someone else and you feel like it really is valuable, maybe it complements what you are doing. It's good to bring that to other people's attention. Either by writing about it or letting people on your list know about it, saying "Hey, this guy's come up with a pretty good product here; it might be interesting to you." The perception is, "I am not so desperate for business that I can't afford to share." So you actually come up ahead of the game by being an unselfish marketer because you are not seen as desperate. You don't ever want to be seen as desperate.

Q. If you don't deal with it, can the feeling of desperation actually turn you into a selfish marketer?

A. Absolutely. Then you have to ask yourself:
- Why am I desperate?
- What is happening that is making me feel this way?
- Is it that I am doing something that isn't working and I need to rethink how I am doing it?
- Am I comparing myself to someone who is much farther down the line so I have unrealistic expectations of myself and am therefore

getting desperate because I am not making the same kind of numbers that somebody else is?

- Have I gotten myself into something that on some level doesn't reflect my values and who I really am?

All of those things can bring about feelings of desperation.

Q. Online networking, offline networking: is one better than the other, do you need both, or is it a matter of personal style and skills?

A. I think it's a matter of personal style and skills. I would certainly say to make use of both of them. But you are going to find that there are some people who are so charismatic and natural in public that offline networking is very, very effective; whereas for someone else the same activity may be just effective. The advantage to online networking is that, for the same amount of time expenditure, you have access to a lot more people but that doesn't mean you are going to form close relationships with all the people. You are going to be able to invite them to see what you are about and they will either find what you are doing as attractive or not.

Certainly a combination is good, if at all possible. You can meet people online. If you go to a live event where you meet them in person, and you have already developed a relationship with them online, then there is a solid friendship there. And it's fun! On top of everything else, when you work only online it is an isolated thing. So coming into contact with the real person takes you out of that isolation. I think we all need that from time to time.

You and I met over dinner at an event in Portland. Here

we are doing this interview. Those kinds of things – we probably would have done it anyway, but there's more meaning behind it now. Earlier when we were getting ready for this call, you said, "It's nice when you are doing this with a friend." That's one of the nice side benefits of networking; it's not just business; you are actually making really good friends along the way.

Q. How do you attract quality people into your network who might be good power partners, peer advisors or joint venture partners? People you can trust your referrals to, or people who might refer others to you?

A. I believe the secret to attracting quality people is by being absolutely transparent and honest about what it is that you are attracting them to. So, if you are attracting them to a business and there are certain things that are going to be required; like let's say they are starting an Internet business, it's a lot of work. You can certainly ease the learning curve for them, but it's still going to be a lot of work. If you present it otherwise, you are going to attract people who are looking for the easy way. But if you are perfectly honest with how much time it really takes, then you are going to be able to attract the people who are willing to do that because you have given them a clear picture of exactly what they are getting into. I think that's what makes the difference. You being honest about what it is, what it takes, what the good things are, what the bad things are, what they can anticipate. Then you are going to attract a higher quality person. And model it; do it! Be a leader and do the things that you are talking about doing. Even if you are in the middle of learning and doing, you don't already have to be a power player. You just have to be doing what you are learning because you are going to be a step ahead of somebody, and that somebody is going to need your help. You are going to be speaking

COACHING COGNITION

their language more because they are near the same level you are.

So if I want someone to become a coaching student, I don't want them to come in because they think that if they sit in a class that they are going to make millions of dollars as a coach. I want them there because they really want to develop those skills, the coaching skills, either for themselves in their personal lives or as a vehicle to help their business. I want them to have a strong motivation for why they are there; because then I know that they will show up for class, they are going to do the assignments, they are going to be ready, and they are going to get a lot out of the program, which is why I am there. I want them to get a lot out of the program. So I won't advertise it and say, "Oh, this is a piece of cake." I will say it's fun, because I think it is, and that's the feedback that I get from the students; that they have fun. But I am not going to say, "You can do this maybe half an hour a week." No! The training class is an hour so it's going to take longer than that.

Q. **Does letting go of any emotional expectation of a sale, or personal agenda from a networking interaction, free you to have a more successful interaction?**

A. I believe it does. Other successful people in the sales industry also confirm this. One really successful sales person I talked with, who does live sales, said that whenever he walks into a customer's office he always carries a roll of money in his pocket to remind himself that he doesn't need the sale. The sale will happen if it is right for that customer. It just puts him in a mindset. I think that when what you are trying to do is to find out "Is this going to address the need of the person I am talking to?" you are probably going to make the sale if it does address the need. But if you are going in with the idea, "If I don't make five more sales by the end of the month, I am not going to reach my goal!" your focus is in the wrong place. Your focus has to be "What is best for this particular person I am talking to right now?" And if you are willing to say, "You know what? I don't think this is right for you, but I do know another product by somebody else that may be a better fit. Let me write down their name." Maybe that customer doesn't buy from you that day, but they are the person that will come back to you another day, because they know they can trust you. You are not in it for just you; you are in it to really help them. I get those kinds of calls where people know that I will make money if they buy something and yet they will ask me my opinion of whether or not it is right for them. They know that I won't say "Oh, by all means you have to do this!" if I don't really believe, from what I have found out about them, that it's going to help them.

> *"The friendships and the idea of building my business through helping other people as they build theirs, is very, very satisfying."*

Q. What have been the biggest rewards for you from your networking activities?

A. The friendships. I have met people all over the world that I deeply cherish. The *Coaching Cognition* program wound up becoming sort of the ultimate networking group because not only did it put groups of people together on a weekly basis over an extended period of time, but it was a unique setting because we talked about things that normally you wouldn't share with people. We talked about values, challenges, and things on a much deeper level than you normally would if you had just met somebody at an event for a couple of days. Out of that came some very, very strong connections that are still continuing. A lot of business partnerships also grew from it. The friendships and the idea of building my business through helping other people as they build theirs, is very, very satisfying. Networking is what brought those people to our doors.

Q. What have been your biggest challenges?

A. The first was, as I've said, when I started my business I gave a lot. I gave my time, I gave my effort, I gave my support; all of that for free. I coached one on one with a lot of people for free. I was still learning and it was an important part of my growth. But it was very difficult for me to make the transition from giving my time away to charging for my time because there came a point where, if I was going to be able to continue, I was going to have to be able to make a living at it. So the reality is that you've got to charge at some point, but this was hard for me.

Then the second thing that was difficult for me, or challenging, was when I couldn't meet one on one with all the people I had been able to meet with before. I had to spend time developing programs and teaching classes. But teaching the classes kind of took the place of that. I missed getting to talk with people one on one. I still got to talk with them; it was just in a different space.

Then the last challenge for me personally was developing myself, not as a leader, because I have always been a leader. It was making the switch from thinking that I could be a powerful business owner, to knowing that I could be a powerful business owner, and then the big switch was to actually be one. I don't mean when the company got to a certain point, but when it became internally a part of my identity; knowing that I can do this! So when a challenge comes up, I am now in a mindset that says "This is part of business and I

Barbara Silva

can handle it because I am who I am!" This took conscious development on my part.

Q. How important are "direct response" marketing skills to attraction marketing or networking professionally? Are they complimentary, necessary, or something completely different?

A. I think it is all part of the follow through. The more different ways that you have of interacting with your potential prospects, the stronger your efforts as a whole are going to be. So I think direct marketing is definitely a piece of that, and that it compliments your networking actions. But I also think it is one of those things where it isn't necessary to use all the different marketing techniques. I think that as your business grows and you have more people working with you, you will probably adopt additional marketing techniques. As you have team members come up and use their natural skills for a certain kind of thing, you may find that you add more techniques. I don't think you have to do it all. Certainly, when you are starting out, you just can't. For me, starting was with social networking online. That was what I was comfortable with; it was natural for me, and that's what got me moving, growing, and established. Now I am free to dabble in some other things. But I am also free to have people that work for me, or with me, who are more expert in the various forms of marketing, take care of that part for me.

Q. Is there anything else you want to share with an aspiring networker or attraction marketer?

A. When you are starting out your business, whatever it is, make sure that the business itself and the business model that you build for yourself is something that you really love. So that it's something that you can put in the amount of time without feeling like you

COACHING COGNITION

are working yourself to death. You need to be able to enjoy it and always know who the person is that you are wanting to network with. Who are the people that you want to meet? Who are the people that you want to attract to your business? What kind of people do you like to hang around with, to socialize with? Keep those people in mind; they are the ones that you want to talk to. If you get a negative response from somebody, or you find that there is somebody who isn't interested in what you are doing, that's okay because they are not the audience you are talking to. So keep yourself focused on the real person that you are talking to. That real person has to be somebody you can see yourself spending time with, whether it's online or offline. Then multiply that person by hundreds, thousands, and then millions. Be very choosy about who those people are going to be and then treat them the way you would treat your own mother or your own child. Treat them as very, very special people.

SUMMARY

- Networking is getting to know people and being able to communicate with them so that both of you come away having benefitted from the exchange
- The secret to attracting quality people is by being absolutely transparent and honest about what it is that you are attracting them to
- You can spam somebody at a dinner party, as well as you can spam them on the Internet
- It is a whole lot easier to talk with people who have requested to talk with you
- A boring networker is one who may have something of value, but they haven't made the connection with how it ties into the needs of the people that they are talking to

BARBARA SILVA

- You've got to charge for your time at some point
- You actually come up ahead of the game by being an unselfish marketer because you are not seen as desperate
- Don't be desperate and think you need the sale. The sale will happen if it is right for that customer
- Relationships can be improved by thinking; what is their problem? What do they need, and how can I provide for that need?
- If you are working with someone else's list, you are ethically bound to treat their list the same way as you would yours
- Learn by doing. Learn by watching what is attractive to you and what isn't.
- A coach can work with you and help you generate ideas, brainstorm and move yourself forward
- Make sure that the business itself and the business model that you build for yourself is something that you really love

BARBARA SILVA'S RECOMMENDED RESOURCES
- *The Renegade Professional* – Ann Sieg and Mike Klingler
- *Romancing the Sale* – Barbara Silva
- CoachingCognition.com
- A good coach (whether through Coaching Cognition or not)

BARBARA SILVA'S RECOMMENDED RESOURCES ONLINE

http://50networkers.com/barbara-silva

COACHING COGNITION

TWO

T he ability to market yourself is a
primary life skill.
**Ann Sieg, The Renegade
Network Marketer**

Ann Sieg's background in athletics, both as a competi-
tor and as a coach for fifteen years, was the genesis of her
passion for finding ways to optimize and improve performance. This passion is not limited to the sports arena, but
later extended to business and marketing which she de-
scribes as a sport for non-athletes.

Ann grew up in a suburb of St. Paul, Minnesota. She attended the College of St. Catherine for one year and then
studied for three years at the University of Minnesota.
Ann had a passion for the health sciences – kinesiology,
physiology, and anatomy as it related to sports medicine
physiology, performance optimization and improvement.
This interest came from being heavily involved in sports
in high school and continued with her being a coach for
fifteen years.

As a young woman, after three weeks of unemployment,
Ann fell into a job working in a nursing home which
helped in her character development. She learned how to
connect with a vulnerable people set – elderly people, and
developed emotional intelligence with the ability to connect to other people at a core level. As a caregiver, Ann
feels that she learned much more from those in her care

than they did from her. She was able to see gifts and talents of the elderly and appreciate them at that level.

Ann's connecting skills integrated well with her later focus on marketing, especially copywriting, where it is essential to connect with people at an emotional level through words. Ann worked with a variety of direct-sales companies over a 22 year period. Initially just focusing on raising her young children and finding a way to make extra money, she achieved strong individual sales success but did not begin building an organization for many years.

In 2002 there was a turning point. Ann began to build a network marketing organization. She continued to achieve sales success as a top performer in her state, and within a five state region, but something was missing. Her organization wasn't seeing the same success and she began to look online for a solution to the problem.

Ann's entry into online marketing in 2005 and later authorship of *The 7 Great Lies of Network Marketing*, *The Renegade Network Marketer* and *The Attraction Marketer's Manifesto* established and strengthened her position as an attraction marketing pioneer.

Q. Has some of your passion for optimization and performance improvement in coaching been useful in preparing you for your later networking and attraction marketing efforts?

A. Enormously! In fact, it came up in a conversation with someone last night when I was thinking about what some might call the "Inner Game"; the mental discipline needed to accomplish goals and overcome the hurdles and challenges when you have to learn something new. I really do attribute my overall success to a lot of mental disciplines. I acquired those primarily through the world of sports, being involved in sports at the level that I was; having a really strong desire to become good at my sport and then working it down to the daily level – what do I need to get done here? What do I need to accomplish? It's all fine to daydream and think about how wonderful and great it would be to be the star of the show, or whatever it may be that someone is wanting to accomplish, but it always comes down to those daily tasks. I get almost religious about it and it's kind of interesting.

Sometimes in life, goals that we want to reach and accomplish have hidden behind them competencies and skill sets that are challenging. Acquiring and building those skills is essential to achieving the goals, but behind that there is a need for developing that "Inner Game" and finding what works for you in order to move you forward through a given process.

Maybe your goal is not something that is easy to accomplish and you've got some mental blocks, whatever they might be. Benchmarking is something that has worked very well for me. That's what I did in sports. I could break it down backwards, looking at the end goal and working backwards from where I wanted to be, to develop a program to get me there. I could look at it and say, "Okay, I want to learn that," or, "Okay, I am weak in my abs or the quads or whatever." And then I would just figure it out and make those connec-

> *"It's all fine to daydream... but it always comes down to those daily tasks."*

tions. In order to learn *that* I am going to have to build up *this* muscle group first. So I just accepted the reality of what I had to do first, and set up a program to accomplish it so I could reach my end goal. The point

ANN SIEG

is that those disciplines have served me well so that I know, overall, when I set out to accomplish something I can do it, I can execute it! I have gone through those processes before, and now I just further refine and systematize them.

Q. When did you first start getting involved in networking and/or attraction marketing?

A. Well, for network marketing, I started more through a direct-sales company when I was pregnant with my second child. I really didn't know what I was falling into, so to speak. Someone had a booth at a parade, and I filled out a form. So there's your lead capture form, it was a piece of paper. I requested a free facial and put it in the drawing. Little did I know that I had just become a lead for someone's business. There's the ethical bribe, getting this free facial, and then next thing you know I am signing up into a very well-known cosmetic company and that's when I got my start. It was multi-level, but more so direct sales.

Q. How long were you involved in networking or attraction marketing before you actually started to see some tangible results for your business?

A. I was in a number of companies throughout the last 22 years. I worked with a number of direct-sales companies where I held home parties and did extremely well just throwing those home parties. So in terms of results, in the retailing and developing a customer base arena, it went very well and I thoroughly enjoyed it. I wasn't focused on building an organization or "downline" at that time. I didn't really know the concept that by doing this I would leverage through their efforts and gain a residual income. There was a little vague and remote understanding of it because the gal who sponsored me was building out a group, but I didn't have an interest to do that myself at the time. My kids were young and I was just really focused on raising my children and then just finding a way to make extra money.

It took on a whole different dimension after I read Robert Kiyosaki's books – *Rich Dad, Poor Dad* and *Cash Flow Quadrant*. I really wanted to get into that B-quadrant and gain leverage through residual income. I got into real estate. Then in 2002, I got into network marketing with a real focus on tapping into residual income and building a down line. I actually did quite well selling products. I was one of the top performers in my state and somewhat in the five-state region as well. As far as my "down-line" goes, they didn't duplicate to the level that I was doing. It seemed like I was doing all the work, so that's when I went online to figure out how to get solutions to that problem. That was in spring of 2004 and by fall of 2005 I was online and starting to generate my own leads. It was a beautiful thing. This was outstanding and made all the difference in the world. From a recent survey I conducted, something like 11% of online marketers are, from what I can gather from my statistical information, performing better than their offline counterparts. I would attribute that to something called leverage, the leveraging you can have through the Internet. So, it's a beautiful thing.

Q. Were there any significant milestones or turning points along the way?

A. I was paying for my leads through the PPC advertising and then sending them out a marketing piece. So it was all fairly expensive. I was building a down line, but it was a rather slow process. Then I thought that I could monetize this whole lead-generation process so I went to the owner of the company I was representing and I was allowed to promote an information product that they had. This was a major breakthrough. Being able to have my prospects fund my marketing and advertising efforts was a major breakthrough. Secondary to this was when I thought, "You know, I can do better than this and I can sell my own information product instead of losing the profits that would go to that particular company." I launched *The Renegade Network Marketer* on June 12, 2007. So those two breakthroughs of being able to monetize the prospecting process of my business were huge.

Q. What makes the difference between an attractive networker, a boring networker and an irritating networker?

A. Beauty lies in the eyes of the beholder, so I think this brings it down to what is the connection between the recipient and the sender. There are enormous dynamics that play out in this. How I might perceive a given message could differ dramatically from how someone else might perceive that message. So I don't think that I would be able to define "Well, this is attractive, this is boring, and this is irritating" carte blanche from the perspective that what I find to be true for those could be very different to somebody else. I will give you an example of this without giving names: The audience I have attracted, as I have done my polling, tends to be baby boomers. I am a baby boomer myself, so I have that baby boomer tone, voice, persona, etc.,

> *"So the goal and the key in understanding your target audience...is having it tailor-made so that it pierces the heart..."*

so those who resonate with this, will more likely find my lesson attractive as opposed to what the baby boomers might be receiving from someone else and thinking, "This person isn't speaking my language. They are boring; they are not connecting with me. This is drivel, meaningless stuff, here!" Or they are irritating to them.

So the goal and the key in understanding your target audience, knowing how to craft your message, is having it tailor-made so that it pierces the heart "Wow, I love this!" The focus needs to be on the prospect and what makes them feel like, "Wow, this person just walked into my life at the most opportune time. They resonate with me, they fulfill my need, and I love them!" When marketers know their audience, are mindful of the dynamics involved, and understand how a message is crafted – that's an ideal world in marketing.

My message wouldn't hit, or resonate so well perhaps, with a different target audience within my niche. It's a big niche. There are different value sets amongst the younger group, say 20 year olds, so it's just really being aware of the dynamics of how you craft a message that is tailor customized for the end recipient. This makes the difference between generally being attractive or not to that particular recipient.

Q. What kind of things have you done consciously to improve your networking skills?

A. One thing I do a lot of – I am doing it literally right now – I am taking notes. I am constantly taking notes and then I do a lot of reflection and thinking back. I will give you a perfect example: as I move into a given project, I will work to set up protocols, procedures, standard operating procedures – basically following a template. For example, when I put together *Renegade Marketing* I was very mindful of this at the onset; this is going to be my procedure – boom, boom, boom. I would put them up on a document and after each session, I would reflect back and optimize my procedure looking for ways to create efficiencies within my business, my mind and capabilities. How can I streamline this? How can I be faster? How can I be better?

When I approach a given project that is what I do. I don't go into it in a random fashion. It is always very focused, very calculated, and very mapped out. I use a variety of tools. I use Mind Meister, for example. I lay it out because I always want to get better and better at my competencies. So, after each session, I would change my document. I tweaked it up, then next time, and next time, and next time. That was how I was able to slice the project up into many protocols, if you will, but then afterwards I would do the same thing and look back at the full project. What worked? What didn't? What could have been better? What did I learn from this? I set up templates to evaluate all facets of my business. I don't have this nailed down in every part though.

There are all different kinds of facets. Something I am always striving to do is streamline. When I run into a hurdle and something isn't working, or I want to better optimize it, I think "I need to go out and get some more resources on this because I missed the mark here in setting up my protocol and I want it to be better optimized". So I go out, read up on a bunch of books or buy courses, whatever is needed.

The most important criteria are those for monetization; cash flow. So if I need to optimize a particular procedure as it relates to monetization, I go out and improve my protocols. This is a very conscientious activity that I do.

Q. **Do you have any particular recommended training resources, books, classes, anything like that which**

come to mind?

A. For attraction marketing, there is so much that formulates into this; I think it was pretty interesting when you were talking about what's attractive, what's boring, what's irritating. Anything that helps me to better understand my audience and be better able to convey messages to my audience; to be more effective in this; to better educate people – all these types of things. I definitely focus on copywriting. It's the ability to persuade someone to my point of view, to help people break through with the material they want to learn as a result of their involvement with me. So I study up on specific copywriters; Gary Halbert, Gary Bencivenga, Clayton Makepeace, Frank Kern. I love Perry Marshall. He is not straight out a copywriter, but his tone and voice and his material are great.

As it relates to attraction marketing, it's learning how to bring someone in as a customer and above and beyond a customer, as a client – someone involved with me at a higher level. So the whole big picture of what formulates into this is basically drawing them in closer to me through persuasion, through the art of copywriting and bringing them closer in through that sales funnel to become a part of my business.

Q. Are there any particular mistakes people make that are unforgivable in networking?

A. I suppose there are but I do not want people to become paralyzed from fear of making a mistake. You've got to get over that hurdle pretty fast or you are never going to grow because you will make mistakes. I call them learning lessons. An unforgivable failure is when you cause irreparable damage to your list; to your relationship with the people on your list. If you do something that is so unethical, so out of character, so self-serving that you've lost complete trust with your list, I would say that is probably the unforgivable – where they cannot forgive you. Whether it was something idiotic, or by design, or something you do as a marketer that is deemed unforgiveable.

What is unforgivable for one person, another person could say, "Eh, whatever." If you run your business so terrified of offending someone, you won't have a business because inevitably in marketing, you are going to offend someone. If not, you don't have enough differentiation factors between you and other marketers. In fact, Dan Kennedy speaks to this. I believe these are his words; "If you haven't pissed somebody off by 12 o'clock that day, you're not doing your job!" Now that is pretty hard core. I don't set out every day to do that by any means, but your message is inevitably going to rub someone the wrong way. If you set out to please everybody, you please nobody. So I want to reach out to certain people and those are the people I want to attract to me. If people don't want to do a lick of work, I am probably not going to have the best message for them.

Do I even want to work with someone who launches off in a bunch of swear words because of an email? No. I see that behavior as disqualifying themselves off my list. Whether they ask to be opted off my list or not, we take them off anyways. That same guy may have perhaps a week later gone, "Oh, I just love this." So who knows? People are so temperamental, but you can't run your business based on the full range of temperaments of everybody out there or you will be out of business before you know it.

You do have to develop a thick skin after a while. I mean, *The 7 Great Lies of Network Marketing* was controversial and it definitely raised a storm. Some people loved it and others didn't. It was marketing. It was intended to cause a polarizing effect, and so those who loved it drew closer to me, and the rest who didn't were angry and they went in another direction. Overall, it was very effective. So in marketing, sometimes you have to be kind of gutsy.

Q. Online networking, offline networking: is one better than the other, do you need both, or is it a matter of personal style and skills?

A. I think it is either. Attraction marketing works differently in the offline world. It can typically be more expensive to do this; throw up a brick and mortar business, make sure it's got good traffic flow, test your signs, your banners, this, that, and the other thing. The same principles apply. Do you have an ethical bribe? Are you providing value? All those are there. It just tends to be less leveraged than online. So it's not as though they are completely separate; in fact I think both can work very well integrated together. For myself, as a personal preference, I just don't care to mix business while I am in my offline world. I used to do that. I would be sizing up the cashier and this and that. I was hitting on everybody and anybody. I don't have to do that anymore and there is a big qualifier there – having people come to you versus chasing people down. That's a painful, ugly exercise. I have done it.

Now, you can apply attraction marketing to the offline world and have them come to you, but again, it is probably going to be more expensive and less leveraged. I don't want people coming to my door in a physical setting and that's just personal preference, but you can definitely apply that in the offline world. In the past, I had them coming to me, and I decided that I do not want that happening. I prefer it online. That's me; personal preference!

Ann Sieg

Q. How do you attract quality people into your network who might be good power partners, peer advisors or joint venture partners? People you can trust your referrals to, or people who might refer others to you?

A. People are looking for people who have results. That's how the real world works. Results! So, when you start getting results, people start pounding down your door. It's a good position to be in because you can turn down one opportunity for a different one. You are bombarded with them and that's an enviable position to be in where you can pick and choose because you have results. The size of your list, the relationship with your list, and the amount of sales you have been able to accomplish. The bottom line is; results are really what count, not talking about results. It's about performance. That's how you attract people – not talking it, but walking it.

> *"In terms of referrals, I consider my audience and how I can best serve them. That's my qualifier."*

In terms of referrals, I consider my audience and how I can best serve them. That's my qualifier. Is this going to be something I can put my name behind and provide to my audience? Now, you can go overboard on that because there are so many things to offer any particular audience. The level at which you are making referrals can vary from A to Z. A promotional email is a referral, and if you feel that it is legitimately a resource that you can recommend to your audience that is going to serve their needs, then this is pretty much the qualifier. It is based not so much on me, but on the audience. As long as they are feeling like, "You know what? This person is really being a great solutions provider for me. They are giving me the stuff that I need. I trust this person." But let's say you pitch something to them and it's just a total bomb; the service was awful. This will damage your relationship with your list.

Q. If results are what really matters, and that is what gets you into that amiable position where you have multiple options to choose from, where do you start if you are just starting out and you don't have any results yet?

A. You've got to start with lead generation. Start generating your own traffic. Traffic generation is about as basic as it gets, and yet I know that is a lot of work right there. It is one thing to get traffic; it's another thing to get traffic into your funnel. For example: you've got a blog with Google Analytics running on it. You are tracking the people coming through and you are seeing a lot of activity, but you don't know anything about an opt-in box for people to receive your newsletter, or you've got the opt-in box down below the fold, or whatever is happening there, and nobody is opting in. Well, straight from the gate you are not getting any results for your efforts. You've got to know what you are doing when you are setting out to do traffic generation.

But it's all a sequential process; it starts there. Are you getting traffic to your blog, to your squeeze page, when you are doing pay per click? Are eyeballs getting on it and are eyeballs doing something about what they are seeing once there? That is the name of the game! It starts at a small level with keenness and an eye towards needing to move people to action. Then you go, "Okay, this is cool. I made that change and two people opted in today. Okay. I am going to see if I can optimize this and see if I can get four people opting in." The crux of direct-response marketing is getting people to take action on your offer. Why should they read your blog post over somebody else's?

We are not just in the information age, we are in the attention age and getting people's attention is becoming more and more difficult to do. Once you start getting in the game you start to see nuances and patterns and it becomes easier to see how to grab people's attention. You've got to get in there, but you've got to understand what you want to accomplish in getting specific actions; measurable actions. Those are the results.

Let's say you start getting some leads and you are converting them, so then you move it up a level and use other strategies and nuances at that stage. But it can go bad right away when a person who has never generated a lead starts hitting on an experienced "heavy hitter" trying to sell them their deal. The "heavy hitter" will be thinking, "What in the world do you bring to the table here? You have a deal and do you know how many other thousand people have that same deal? Why am I supposed to be interested in yours? Come again?" So your deal, your opportunity, isn't what makes you great; what makes you great is the ability to convert, converting people in your sales funnel.

Q. **You touched on "direct response" methods there. How important are "direct response" marketing skills to attraction marketing or networking professionally? Are they complimentary, necessary, or something completely different?**

A. I would consider them necessary. I play to win. I don't want to mess around and just do busy work that doesn't lead to direct results, so you have to understand the underlying dynamics of what leads to a sale. Twitter, as an example – do you have a link that leads somewhere? Does it go to your Facebook page with a little blurb about something that then leads to another link and you are moving them down a slope so to speak; your sales funnel, to ultimately make a decision to do business with you? This is integral to attraction marketing: leads reading through your email copy and liking the message, hitting the link to join up for your webinar and then you host your free webinar, let's say, and then there is an exit survey or an offer with a link. It's integral; I wouldn't do it any other way. It would just be an endeavor without any way to calculate what my actions are yielding.

Q. Does letting go of any emotional expectation of a sale, or personal agenda from a networking interaction, free you to have a more successful interaction?

A. I think it can be done in a very cheesy way. You can hear the cheesy sales lingo – and that's something I really ask people to pay attention to when they are going through a sales experience. Is the sales rep pulling out really canned lines where they assume the sale? And you are thinking "Don't even go there buddy; that line is so old!" I have taken lots and lots of sales training, so I may be a little more savvy to pick these up. To me it doesn't seem very authentic or like they are serving me. They are actually being self-serving and their underlying problem is that they are unskilled in knowing how to better connect my wants and needs to their offer. They are resorting to cheesy sales techniques, little one-liners that you can read right through, you might feel "This isn't cutting it for me. You are not serving my wants, and in fact, are not even listening to me."

Now on the other hand, it really depends on the audience and who you are working with. In my industry, there is a real lack of leadership. People are looking for leadership and people who are able to demonstrate that. People can sense "Alright, we are moving to a sale." They can sense when someone has, a non-abusive, non-manipulative way in terms of their leadership. In leadership that is, "You know what? I trust

Ann Sieg

this person and they are taking me to the right place."

I can do that with confidence at my level. I can confidently tell someone what they need to do in order to reach success because I can speak to it due to the results I have reached. People are craving that leadership and confidence backed by results in my industry for what I am "selling". So in some regards I do assume the sale because I know what I am talking about and can say "Ignore my advice to your folly" in an authoritative way, knowing that someone will step up to the plate. Not in an arrogant way, but in a way that will make someone sit up and pay attention: "This person has the goods so I better move forward with this decision."

That's just putting it into context. It really depends on the audience. With my audience, I sell a product, but what I am really selling is trust and credibility because people are moving forward with decisions that are quite a bit different than the dynamics of buying a dishwasher. Buying into my method, my way of doing things, my way of marketing is causing big shifts in the way people think and conduct themselves; first the way they think and then their behavioral outcomes. So I am working at the way they think, and am persuading them to my point of view. That is really what I am selling them.

> "... what I am really selling is trust and credibility..."

Q. What have been the biggest rewards for you from your networking activities?

A. I gain tremendous satisfaction from working with people and moving them into a new model, a new way of understanding things, all with an eye towards what is going to work better for them. What is going

THE RENEGADE NETWORK MARKETER

to be more productive? What is going to be the net effect here? That's why, in my years of educating and
teaching, it was always to break things down to the
level where the person could comprehend, understand, and implement so that they could get a better
outcome and result. That is enormously satisfying and
it's something I just get this great fascination and intrigue with. How can I break this down even more?
There's a road block here – I need to break it down
even more. There's a gap here – how can I fill that gap?
I guess it's that intrigue with helping people connect
the dots in their processes so that they can ultimately
get better results. I know how frustrating it can be to
not get results; it's not a fun place to be, feeling power-
less. I think that is really the net effect of what I want
to accomplish, to bring people into a more empowered
model, even to be able to self-educate and not just rely
on someone dispensing stuff to them. They can go out
and access information in a proactive way.

Q. **What have been your biggest challenges?**

A. When you are running a business, there are so many
competencies to develop. The challenge is just being
mindful of them and the need to put attention towards
one over the other as I weigh them out against other
opportunities. Why should I focus on this one a little
more, this particular competency over that one? There
are so many to learn and with the proficiency needed
in all those respective competencies, you constantly
have to weigh out improving negotiation skills, hiring
skills and team building skills. Even with all that said,
the foundation is marketing, because a dollar earned
today is better than a dollar earned tomorrow. With
that dollar you earned today, you can access resources
to help you develop other competencies. So developing marketing expertise is always the first and primary
directive. I would say this is probably the biggest chal-

lenge – knowing which competency to develop next, to put my focus on.

Q. Is there anything else you want to share with an aspiring networker or attraction marketer?

A. The ability to market yourself is a life skill. Typically, marketing is always related to business and that's primarily who my audience is; people who want to conduct business closed on sales. But marketing your ideas, your beliefs, anything – is a life skill to develop that is going to help you have greater satisfaction in life. You are going to be able to work with more people of like mind when you are able to do that and become a more effective communicator by being able to sell your ideas. You are always selling something; when you are married, when you have children, with teammates. In fact, I teach my teammates this all the time. We are marketing to each other when we have a meeting and you are presenting this idea over that. It is such a primary life skill to acquire.

I have a 19-year-old son whom I have had talks with about this. From an income-building standpoint the playing field has been leveled. People are competing for jobs and business on a global scale now, not just in your community. The thought of this can be either very intimidating or very empowering but it becomes an imperative. In fact, we are putting together a product right now for the Renegade System, working with a very high-level network marketer. He has brought his eight year old son in. His son created a video. He did an amazing video presentation because he has seen his dad do it, watched his dad's videos every day, and is growing up with it. This kid is becoming a darn good marketer at what I would call unconscious competency. He does not have to have this brain-numbing, head-banging experience trying to figure out Internet marketing. He is growing up with it in a really organic fashion. I believe this video is actually going to be in one of our marketing pieces. It becomes a little harder when we find ourselves having to learn this, and we are up there in our later years. We have to deal with technology to even facilitate doing attraction marketing, but it's a skill set that is not going to go away or decrease in need. It's going to be amplified. Welcome to the solution economy. If you are willing to step up to the plate, you can have a piece of it!

Summary

- Ann attributes her overall success to mental disciplines
- Sometimes in life, goals that we want to reach have hidden behind them competencies and skill sets that are challenging
- Find your "Inner Game": what works for you in order to move you forward through a given process
- It always comes down to doing those daily tasks
- Understand leverage through residual income
- Leverage through the Internet can make all the difference
- Consider monetizing the lead generation process by leveraging someone else's product
- Consider further monetizing by creating your own product
- Attraction or irritation is in the eye of the beholder. Know your audience and craft your message tailor-made for them
- Listen to your audience; serve their wants
- Consider your audience and how you can best serve them
- If you set out to please everybody, you please

Ann Sieg

nobody
- Don't go into a project in a random fashion; map it out. Plan, implement and optimize
- You have to understand the underlying dynamics of what leads to a sale
- What Ann is really selling is trust and credibility
- Your deal, your opportunity – isn't what makes you great
- The bottom line is results are really what count, not talking about results. It's about performance
- Results build confidence and allow you to speak with authority
- Ann wants to bring people into a more empowered model, even to be able to self-educate and not just rely on someone dispensing information to them
- The ability to market yourself is a life skill
- Welcome to the solution economy; step up to the plate and have a piece of it!

Ann Sieg's recommended resources
- Mind Meister
- Master Copywriters
    - o Gary Halbert
    - o Gary Bencivenga
    - o Clayton Makepeace
    - o Frank Kern
    - o Perry Marshall
- Your Audience – Listen and learn to understand your own audience
- *The Renegade Network Marketer* – Ann Sieg

Ann Sieg's recommended resources online
http://50networkers.com/ann-sieg

THREE

If you focus on finding ways to help other people, you will have the very first step in becoming successful in any endeavor.

**J. Joshua Beistle,
Founder/CEO My Phone Room**

Josh grew up in the backwoods of Mississippi where his nearest neighbor was a mile away. Around high school age, his family lived in Savannah, Georgia. Even as a teenager, he thought of himself as an entreprenuer. One of his most successful early part-time business ventures was going door to door providing a service spray painting house addresses on curbs.

Josh spent a year in college on a full scolarship, but was impatient to jump into his career and felt college was a waste of time. Not finishing college is something that Josh regrets now that he has the benefit of hindsight. It was the first thing he felt like he ever really failed at. Unlike high school, there was nobody reminding him to do what he needed to do. Josh says that the reason he was not successful in college was because he hadn't taken the responsibility for success into his own hands and made it happen.

His first actual job was as a telemerketer, which he began when he started college. From this he learned a lot about sales and marketing. Josh achieved success in the corporate world with direct response marketing, but didn't have any success with network marketing until he was about thirty.

Beginning in late 2008, Josh began to focus and implement the attraction principles that he had learned. He has since achieved significant "overnight" success with his different businesses and has assumed the moniker "The Attraction King".

Josh is the founder and CEO of MyPhoneRoom.com, a professional call center that handles lead qualification and personal appointment setting for many different businesses.

Q. How long were you involved in networking or attraction marketing before you actually started to see some tangible results for your business?

A. I didn't have any success in network marketing until around 2005. It took me working part-time, years and years. I actually became successful in corporate America in direct response marketing long before I began to understand what networking was all about. I became completely consciously aware of attraction marketing in late 2008, and as I began to implement that, I started to see some massive changes and improvements in my business. I went from adding somewhere around 500 people into my different businesses in 2008 to over 5,000 in 2009! In fact, in January of 2009, I added about 500 people into one company. That's really where it started to take off for me. I came to understand and identify the different aspects of my focus, started communicating this with other people, and asking them to participate in the creative process in accomplishing this goal. By this time I was able to manifest what I would have previously felt was impossible, and basically become what some people would call an overnight success. Though it did take me years and years to get here, what ultimately pushed me over the edge and gave me the momentum to succeed was applying attraction marketing and the "law of attraction".

Q. Significant milestones or turning points?
A. I have always been an entrepreneur. I started with my first network marketing opportunity when I was sixteen. My dad had to sign me up for it because you had to be eighteen to join. For the next five or six years, every few months I was doing one program or another to make money, whether it was stuffing envelopes, trying to do easy crafts from home or take pictures for a living. I always had this idea that I was an entrepreneur. Between network marketing and traditional business and between the ages of sixteen and twenty-five, I probably worked with a hundred different businesses. Most of them didn't turn out to be anything.

I have heard a lot about attraction marketing my entire life, because I studied a lot of personal development material, but I really didn't have the first clue about it until I read the book *The Secret* by Rhonda Byrne. When I read that book, it really exposed me to the idea that we can attract into our universe that which we focus on. I went to the smartest person I know – a gentleman who has mentored me for the last several years – and he turned me onto *The Master Key System* by Charles F. Haanel. Reading *The Master Key System* was like trying to read the Encyclopedia Britannica; it took me months and months to get through it.

Now, as I look back on my life, I realize that in times of great stress, great difficulty or great challenge, I was often able to summon the positive energy, focus, and patience to sit down with a calm head and say, "Let's focus on what we really need. What can we do to

J. JOSHUA BEISTLE

make this happen?" Much of my success in corporate America was using this approach. I was using attraction marketing the entire time, but at the time I didn't realize that's what it was.

Q. What makes the difference between an attractive networker, a boring networker and an irritating networker?

A. I have a lot of love for irritating networkers. I like irritating networkers better than I like boring networkers. I think an irritating networker is somebody who is hounding you all the time to get involved in something, to join their deal, to basically sell you. At least the one good thing an irritating networker has going for them is that they are taking action, and action is a huge part of success. I would think a boring networker is somebody that you don't even notice. This is somebody who is not really doing anything or they are just building and working so slow that there is just nothing interesting there at all.

> *"The attraction marketer, the attraction networker, is somebody who exemplifies leadership, draws people into their organization... by helping others, by being able to share a clear vision, and by doing."*

The attraction marketer, the attraction networker, is somebody who exemplifies leadership, draws people into their organization and into their game by helping others, by being able to share a clear vision, and by doing. There's the law of attraction and then there's attraction marketing, and they have a lot in common. They also have some things that are very specific. The law of attraction is the overall bigger picture. The application of attraction marketing is maybe a micro-version of it.

MY PHONE ROOM

How do I use attraction marketing to get extraordinary results? Well first and foremost, I have a very clear vision of what I am going to accomplish. I can tell you that vision in layman's terms, and it's very important that when you are sharing things with people you do so in simple, bite-sized chunks. I will give you an example: I can tell somebody on the phone that I have a goal to build a really large team this year of at least 15,000 people. A team that is flourishing and growing, where people can interact and participate and help one another and build friendships and relationships that last a lifetime and that's my goal.

Attraction marketing is very simply the fact that you know where you are going, you can express it clearly to other people, and you invite them to join you. You are not compelling them. That is the difference between the attraction marketers and irritating networkers. The irritating ones are trying to drive you along and sell you on their idea of what you should do.

I don't try to compel people into joining me. I disqualify people. I tell people every step of the way that this is probably too much work for them, and there is going to be a lot more involved in it than they really want to do, and I take it away from them. I know where I am going. I invite them to join me, but I invite them to join me through an application process where I begin to ask them what makes them think that they have what it takes, or can learn to grow into what it is going to take, to be successful and be a positive part of my team. At that point I am no longer selling; I am simply attracting and I am giving people an opportunity to participate in what I am doing if they qualify and are working towards it.

Part of the law of attraction is focus. So whether you

are using the law of attraction to focus on things and manifest things in your own reality, or whether you are making your prospect focus on themselves, the process, your opportunity, and where you are going – that in turn actually begins to attract them to what you are doing.

The next thing that I do in attraction marketing, which is a key part of the process, I find out what people want and love to do. Donald Trump says that you should absolutely, without a doubt, do what you love to do, what you would do even if you weren't being paid. If you want to succeed in any endeavor, I believe you must have two things: focus and consistency. Most people end up working on projects and doing things in their life that they literally don't want to do – that's what we call a job. Or they may be working on a business that they are not passionate about. When you are working at something you are not passionate about, discipline has to come into play. If you don't have any discipline and you are not passionate about what you are doing, you won't have the focus and consistency to get anything done. On the other hand, people who love what they do can rely on their passion and enthusiasm and don't have to be disciplined. They are focused and consistent enough to be successful.

> *"If you want to succeed in any endeavor, I believe you must have two things: focus and consistency."*

Once I have invited somebody to be a part of my vision and my team, and they begin to go through that process, I very quickly begin to find out what they really deeply desire. We need to understand that in networking, there is effort and energy that is expended and we are going to have to do some free work – this is

MY PHONE ROOM

not some get rich quick thing – but I need them to tap into and become very focused on what they really want. Once you can get people to say, "Hey, this is what I want; this is what I am hoping for," then whatever the efforts are that are required to succeed in their business, whatever the costs associated with getting started in that business, they all pale in comparison to somebody getting what they want. When what they really want is the reward, the cost of time, effort, energy, money, and resources are always very small, if you can put them on that path.

Not only do I want to attract people to me, but in the process, I get them to focus on what they want. In doing so, I am actually allowing them to tap into the law of attraction so that they too can begin to move towards their goals.

I can take this one step further and say that once I learned everything at the basic level, in order to really grow as quickly as I wanted to grow, I not only needed to begin to attract other people to me, but other people of specific caliber. So what I began to do was attract leaders to me because I was focusing on leaders and I was putting my focus and my energy towards attracting other leaders. I would end up on the phone with other leaders who had organizations, who had a strong share of influence and not necessarily leaders in network marketing or any specific endeavor, but just leaders in life. When I began to attract leaders, I began to enjoy attraction marketing on steroids, because now I had this incredible leverage. I was now attracting people who had instantly gone out and with their influence, shared my message and my vision with so many more people in such a short period of time. So, that's been my strategy this past year and a half and the results have been awesome.

J. Joshua Beistle

Q. Are there any particular mistakes people make that are unforgivable in networking?

A. I think unforgivable is a very strong term. I would like to think that as long as we have another remedy, we will have another opportunity to do what's right and make good decisions. As it relates to networking, there is no doubt that if you put your own needs before others, if you gain a reputation as being greedy, or if you don't try to help others, then perhaps that is as close as you can get to unforgivable. A big part of attraction marketing, and a big part of the law of attraction marketing, is your reputation. You can never really attain leverage with attraction marketing if you are taking advantage of people along the way. There are some who just don't get that and it's unfortunate, but I have always held the view that if I can't help somebody accomplish their goals and needs first, then I don't deserve anything in return.

Now you can't help everyone. You can't want something for someone else more than they want it for themselves. That's very important because most people are going to fail in life. I look at my team and I see many times that half the people are achieving and half that aren't. Those who aren't succeeding are not focused in taking the actions that they need to take to be successful. I have to harden myself against wanting it for them more than they want it for themselves. But having said that, don't be greedy, and put others needs in front of yours.

> *"...if I can't help somebody accomplish their goals and needs first, then I don't deserve anything in return."*

Q. Online networking, offline networking: is one better than the other, do you need both, or is it a matter of

MY PHONE ROOM

personal style and skills?

A. Here's a little analogy to answer this question. What key things do you need to make a great cherry pie? You need really good, sweet cherries, you need a great pie-crust recipe, and you need the loving care of someone to prepare and bake it. If you want to be successful in marketing, whether it is online marketing or offline marketing, you too need good ingredients to create a successful marketing campaign. The key ingredients are these: you must have good leads and/or good prospects. You must have the understanding that the next step is to work those leads through a relationship process because people like to do business with people they know, like, and trust. Without relationships there is nothing. It is not so much where the marketing comes from, from a statistical standpoint, as much as the marketer working the data with the goal to create relationships.

The last ingredient in a successful marketing process is leverage – to be able to sift and sort with quickness and ease so you are not wasting time with the wrong people. One thing that happens online is that it is so much easier for prospects to become distracted than offline. If someone is getting a post card at home, there may be five or six other pieces of mail there to look at and a few magazines in the room, but if they are online, there's a thousand, a million other websites that they are going to go to and click on. It is important to note that it's less likely for prospects to remember you unless you use really strong marketing principles to make yourself memorable. That's why a lot of people have said that attraction marketing is about putting your picture up; to make yourself and what you are doing prominent enough to where people can really connect, remember and see what you are doing.

Q. **How important are "direct response" marketing skills to attraction marketing or networking professionally? Are they complementary, necessary, or something completely different?**

A. I would say that they are complementary. If someone is to the point that they understand that we all have a sphere of influence that is either positive or negative, that we are either exerting influence or being influenced, I would say that my direct marketing skills complement my businesses. But I am seeing ten-fold the response through attraction marketing, through networking, through people I am being introduced to, than I am through direct-response marketing. There are people who are just getting started, people who haven't built a sphere of influence, or their relationship with their potential sphere of influences is upside down for whatever reason – whether they just are not there yet from a personal development standpoint or perhaps they have misused or abused their sphere of influence in the past. For these people, direct-response marketing is not just complementary, it's mandatory. It is the only way for them to go out and build a new sphere of influence.

Sometimes you have to start with leads and build relationships, and then as you gain some success, you can go out and generate prospects on your own and then build relationships from there. Then over time, what will inevitably happen is that you will have a core team and that core team, through their own efforts of direct-response marketing and their sphere of influence connections, will begin to bring you and introduce you to new people. At that point, you will essentially be able to work without the constant need of direct-response marketing because eventually you won't have time for anything else but the relationships that are being brought to you.

Q. Is there anything else you want to share with an aspiring networker or attraction marketer?

A. Perhaps the very best advice that was ever given to me is if you focus on finding ways to help other people, you will have the very first step in becoming successful in any endeavor. All success has to do with flow and the way that you achieve a positive flow of funds coming to you, of abundance, of positive energy, of material things – it all comes from positioning yourself between people and what they want and helping them as a guide to get from where they are to where they want to be.

When you begin to see yourself in that way, and when you stop selling and stop wanting it for them more than they want it for themselves, then you have taken the very first steps towards a complete paradigm shift that will lead to the biggest breakthroughs in your entire career.

For me, attraction marketing has been where I just stop trying to force it to happen and I just started really being clear about my vision, about where I was going to go, and I just said, "You know what? If you want to come with me, to be honest I don't know if you are qualified, but I can put you through an application process. I will see if this is something we could accept you on, but I don't know. Here is where I am going to go, though!" People want to be a part of something and if you can give them that opportunity to be a part of something, then you have taken the first step in learning how to do attraction marketing.

Tony Robbins says that you become powerful in your moment of decision – somewhere along the lines you are going to have to make a decision to stop worrying about yourself and focus on finding ways to help oth-

J. JOSHUA BEISTLE

er people. When you do that you become powerful in your ability to use attraction marketing to better your networking business. I think that's my final thought.

MY PHONE ROOM

SUMMARY

- People often work years and years before becoming an overnight success
- What ultimately gave me the momentum to succeed was applying attraction marketing and the "law of attraction"
- Attraction marketing and "the law of attraction" are not the same thing, but they do have things in common
- Attraction marketing is very simply the fact that you know where you are going, you can express it clearly to other people, and you invite them to join you. You are not compelling them
- It all comes from positioning yourself between people and what they want and helping them as a guide to get from where they are to where they want to be
- Sometimes you have to start with leads and build relationships
- Where the marketing comes from is not so much what matters; without relationships there is nothing
- Make a decision to stop worrying about yourself and focus on finding ways to help other people
- Don't be greedy, and put others needs in front of yours
- You can't want something for someone else more than they want it for themselves
- Successful people take the responsibility for success into their own hands and make it

happen
- You should absolutely, without a doubt, do what you love to do, and what you would do for free

J.Joshua Beistle's recommended resources
- *The Secret* – Rhonda Byrne
- *The Master Key System* – Charles F. Haanel

J.Joshua Beistle's recommended resources online
http://50networkers.com/j-joshua-beistle

J. Joshua Beistle

FOUR

Having that genuine interest in someone, that's attractive!

**Gene Hamilton, Founder/CEO,
I Take The Lead**

Gene Hamilton is the CEO and founder of *I Take The Lead*, a 10 year old leads group organization with about 100 leads groups in Oregon, Seattle and Denver. Gene started the organization in 1999 in the Portland area where they now have about 60 leads groups. Through leads groups, Gene and his team provide an introduction service introducing people who want to do business with people who want to get business done.

This is quite a ways from his beginnings as a farm boy from southern Iowa who joined the Air Force where he worked on air-to-air and ground-to-ground missiles. Gene often jokes that these were great transferable skills if he wanted to be a terrorist or an arms merchant. But it was electronics training, which led him to doing college training on computers. Gene worked with computers for six years before moving into the insurance industry.

After twelve years of selling insurance, Gene started his current venture; building leads groups and helping to facilitate professional networking between business people. He feels that his 22 years in *Toastmasters*, building new Toastmasters groups, was a networking activity and although it is an all-volunteer organization – he developed transferable skills that helped with I Take The Lead.

GENE HAMILTON

Q. How long were you involved in networking and going to leads groups before you actually started to see some tangible results for your business?

A. With insurance, it is pretty quick. For large ticket items, it can take six months to a year for some people. With other people it takes six to nine months to make their first sale, and then things take off. Every person is different.

One big thing that affects results is how much you are interacting with other people so that they trust you. If you sit back on your hands waiting for business to come, sometimes it doesn't come and sometimes it does. The big thing with leads groups is that you need to give to get. You have to pass leads to other people in the leads group so they know they can trust you. Plus, there is a factor there of, "Boy, Gene has given me a lot of leads. I don't want him to leave the group because he is frustrated. I want to make sure I give him some leads back." So, it's reciprocal. Basically it's give to get. You really should give three to four leads for every lead you receive in return. It's not one for one.

Q. How long were you doing networking before you would say that you were proficient at it, could do it professionally, and build an attractive network?

A. This is a really a hard question because I feel like I get better every day. I get a new idea or I learn a new trick. To be a good networker could take years, literally.

You may not be good today, but to round out your skills and learn something new is really important. This is why we have speakers come into our groups and give new ideas; to help make people better. As your team gets better, the 15-20 people you are networking with every week in the group, it's a win-win situation for everybody. It is a work in progress. I can always be better, so I'm always learning, and learning new techniques.

Q. **A lot is said about having a catchy 30-second elevator speech that you can deliver confidently. How important is this? How can this be used to attract interest instead of being categorized and dismissed?**

A. I think it is very important. If you have 10 to 50 people in a room and everyone does their 30-second commercial, most of them are just going to blend together. If you have something that reaches out and grabs you, it is going to make a big difference. They call it an elevator speech because if you get on an elevator with someone and go up to the 15th floor, you have about 30 seconds to give that person a message and say, "Hey, we need to talk." Because, they are going to get off the elevator and you are probably never going to see them again.

You need something that hooks their attention and says, "Wow! I need to talk to you and get your business card." That's the whole point – it doesn't matter if you are in an elevator, passing somebody on the street, in the grocery line, or in a leads group, or in a chamber of commerce meeting. You want to say something that is going to hook several peoples' attention and say, "I need to talk to Gene because he's got something that might be of interest to me." So, I think it's very, very important. You want it to shock people or get their attention. For instance, one person says, "I'm with the CIA." And people go, "What?", "The Clackamas Insurance Agency." Everybody laughs, but everyone remembers that person.

The other day there was a banker. He looked like Mr. Laced-Up-Buttoned-Down tie sort of guy and with

GENE HAMILTON

a straight face, he says, "I'm Batman." Everybody cracked up because it was totally out of context for him. Having something that is unique like that, which will catch people's attention – something that will stick in their mind so if they don't talk to you now, they will look you up later and say, "Hey, I want to talk to you." I think it's extremely important. You've got to cut yourself out of the crowd and make yourself unique.

Q. **What makes the difference between an attractive networker, a boring networker and an irritating networker?**

A. A boring networker is Mr. or Ms. Milquetoast. You walk away going, "There is really not much there. It's just vanilla and it's really not much different than the next person that comes along." The irritating networker is one who, even though you told him 15 times you are not interested, are still trying to sell you or shove their product down your throat. An attractive networker is someone who really takes an interest in you.

One of our members says a good way to attract someone is to say, "Hey, I'd like to sit down and have a cup of coffee with you so I can know better how to pass you leads and get business for you." If you have that genuine interest, "I know I can get you some business. I'm out there doing a lot of networking and I'm going to run into people that need your business"; that is attractive! Somebody is more likely to say "Wow! I want to talk to you because I think we could be good for each other." It's a two

> *"A boring networker is Mr. or Ms. Milquetoast. You walk away going, 'There is really not much there'..."*

I TAKE THE LEAD

way street.

Q. What kind of things have you done to improve your networking skills?

A. A lot of different things. Reading books is a big one. I read a lot of books. *The Referral of a Lifetime* by Tim Templeton and *Endless Referrals* by Bob Burg come to mind. There are dozens of books available along the lines of networking and that sort of thing. Taking classes and listening to speakers who are really good, is another. People laugh when I sincerely say that the 30th, 40th, or 50th time I've heard them talk, I'm still learning something. They are reminding me of something I forgot. Sometimes I hear something in a different way, or something they never talked about before, but it just comes out in that one speech. It is good to hear them speak again because I might pick up something new that I could utilize in order to help people out.

Q. If you are in a group that you see frequently, do you always use the same speech or do you have several that you rotate?

A. I think it is important to have 5-15 different commercials. You probably want a 10-15 second commercial if you are at a chamber function where, say there are 200 people there, and they are only going to give you 10-15 seconds to speak. It would be rude to try to do a 60 second one with a big crowd like that. So, you need a 10-15 second commercial. You also need a 30 second one, and a 60 second one. You do need to change it around because if you are saying the same thing every week and meeting you go to, it gets old. But, then again you have taglines that people always say. We had a gentleman who is "not your ordinary bean counter" and everybody laughs because it is funny. Then, he could pause and say, "Not your..." and stop and then everybody else goes, "ordinary bean counter," because people are expecting that. You are getting the audience to play along and listen. These are all good things to have.

Q. What is more important, your skills, your personality, posture, being able to provide value to people, being a good listener or having that 30-second speech? To be a great networker, is there something that is more important?

A. Sincerity, genuineness, and the ability to listen and show interest in the other person. Your 30-second commercial and all of that is important too, but really, people don't care how much you know until they know how much you care. People do business with people they know, like and trust. By creating that trust and rapport; these are huge.

Listen more than talking. Jack, our sales trainer, calls it the "dummy curve." We start off not knowing what we are doing, so we don't talk very much; we listen. We are really effective at doing that. Then, as we get more confident we start to talk more. This is not as effective because we're just throwing up all over our clients with product knowledge. We need to go back up the dummy curve and be talking less and listening more. Ask questions; find out what the person is really interested in. This shows that you care and are not just trying to sell something.

Q. If I was just starting out with my brand new company or as a new associate or employee for an established company, what is the best use of time initially to start developing my networking skills?

A. I would say, calling people that you know and trying to hook up with them. Saying, "I'd like to come over." A lot of companies do that. Pick the people you know and try them out because you know they are safe. You go and practice your spiel on them and if they want to buy, that's great. If not, you let them know up front that you just wanted someone to practice on. Going to mixers and networking events; there are tons of them around town. You can find out by going on Meet-up and similar sorts of places online. A lot of them don't cost anything.

Go out and start talking to people. Again, show a genuine interest in them; about what they are doing and say, "Hey, I'm new to the business, but maybe I could tell you about it." Just to practice. I don't think most people will really object to that. They will want to help you out. They want to like you, and see you succeed. So, that's a way for you to practice in a safe environment, rather than knocking on doors.

Q. So, as long as you're genuine and you give them permission to not be interested?

A. Absolutely. If somebody thinks you are going to shove it down their throat, selling some kind of insurance or product that they don't really want, of course they don't want it; they don't know what it is! Instead say, "I'd like to tell you about it so I can practice." At the end say, "What did you think?" If they say "I'd like to buy it", great! If they say "I'd like to know more about it." You genuinely say, "Well, that's great. Thank you. I don't expect you to buy this. Don't feel pressure." There are different schools of thought, but that's what I prefer.

Q. Are there any particular mistakes people make that are unforgivable in networking?

A. Anything is probably forgivable, but the key one you don't want to make is being too forceful. Over the last 10 years, we have met thousands of realtors and finan-

GENE HAMILTON

cial planners and the next guy or gal that comes along says "I want to be your financial planner. I want to be your realtor." It's really annoying when they repeatedly, don't take "no" for an answer.

> *"It's not the person that gets the most leads or business cards who wins; it's the person who creates the most meaningful relationships."*

Some people think, "Well, if I just keep dogging them long enough, they will eventually buy something from me." It's just annoying. You don't want to be annoying. You don't want to be irritating to people. The other thing that is not very endearing is, "I want to tell you about my product, but I could really care less about what you do." At a minimum you should probably take some interest in their product so you can at least know what you can do for them.

Q. Was there any point in your networking career where you thought "this is something special"?

A. I really enjoy what I do. I enjoy meeting new people and having the prospect of meeting all kinds of people. Some become members and some don't. Some you become friends with and whether they join or not, it's a lot of fun.

Q. Obviously you like the leads group and the mixers. Are there any other kinds of networking activities you do, or prefer? What have you found to be useful?

A. The larger the event is not necessarily the better thing. One of our members is fond of saying "It's kind of fly-by or drive-by networking".

Getting 50, 75, 100 business cards from an event that

I TAKE THE LEAD

are going to be thrown into a drawer really doesn't work. It's not the person that gets the most leads or business cards who wins; it's the person who creates the most meaningful relationships. Getting three to four business cards and names of people you are going to follow up with, and possibly create lasting relationships, is a lot more valuable.

Q. Online networking, offline networking: is one better than the other or is it a matter of personal style and skills?

A. I think it's a matter of personal style and how comfortable you are with people. If you are not a big face-to-face person, then online might be more valuable for you. The next generation is big on texting and email and this is okay, but networking is still a personal activity. I find that it is the face-to-face networking that really gets the job done.

Q. Do you find social media to be a distraction or a benefit for your business?

A. It has really become a huge phenomenon. I don't do it as much as I should. Some of it I find really annoying like, "Hey I'm going to go have a ham sandwich or take a nap." I really don't care. That kind of stuff is too much information. But, for people wanting to ask you stuff or get information, it can be a lot of fun. Huge corporations are hiring people to field calls and questions for them; it has to be of value to them.

Q. Do you ever feel overwhelmed with all of the things you had to learn or improve on to achieve the success you desired? If so, how did you work through that?

A. Constantly. When you have 100 leads groups out there it is really hard to maintain them. If all of them went away at once, that would be the worst case scenario. That's not going to happen because people find value

GENE HAMILTON

and there are always going to be people coming and going. With the anxiety gone that they all could leave, what's the next worst thing? A whole group could leave. They do that sometimes, but not very often. After this, the next worst thing is if somebody quits. This is not really a big thing though. You're kind of sad about it because you really liked Joe or Mary, they are nice people. You are sorry they are leaving, but they are.

We always have a lot of new people coming in. This is one big source of anxiety. It's an overwhelming prospect to deal with all these people. But, you set up systems and try to make it work out and it does basically.

Q. How important is it to be clear on your personal and business core values in relating to people in a networking context?

A. I think it's critical. If you are doing a lot of things that don't match up with your core values, at some point in time it is going to create a lot of havoc for you. If you sincerely believe you are accountable and aren't accountable, or believe you are ethical and what you are doing is not really ethical, it is quicksand. It is not going to give you long-term success. If you do a lot of things you aren't very comfortable with, at some point in time anxiety will build up to the level where you go "I'm out of here!" So, building your values, skills and ethics into your business I think is extremely important.

> *"Treat everyone with integrity and treat them like you would expect to be treated."*

Q. What are some of your values that help you communicate effectively with people and attract interested

prospects, and avoid or minimize offending people, especially your family, friends and neighbors?

A. Treating everyone with integrity and treating them like you would expect to be treated. Not everybody wants to be treated the way you want to be treated. But, I think most people do.

Show a lot of empathy for people when they are busy or financially strapped. People want to be treated with honesty, integrity and a caring attitude. Fortunately, most of our people are like that. Everyone is pretty ethical and caring, and they are out there helping each other. Be careful that you aren't creating a big can of worms in which you mix a bunch of ethical people with a bunch of unethical ones. *If you generally try to work with ethical caring people*, I think it makes for a lot less fireworks and a lot less problems than if you have that mixed bag.

Q. Does letting go of any emotional expectation of a sale, or personal agenda from a networking interaction, allow for you to have a more successful interaction?

A. I think so. If you want to join great, but if you don't want to that's great too. If people leave after a while, this is OK, because it's not working out for them. This is not a one size fits all. You have to expect that there will be some rejections and disappointment. It's part of the game. We try to help people be better at what they are doing so they are successful. But, it's a mixed bag. You don't really want to have that expectation that you are going to sell somebody something when you talk to them.

Q. How do you handle fear of rejection?

A. I think one thing is not having huge expectations that you are going to make a sale or that people are go-

Gene Hamilton

ing to join. "Sales", in general, is a rejection kind of world. There are a lot of rejections and you prepare yourself for them so you aren't let down. It's always disappointing when someone you really like leaves. Or, you have someone as your customer and all of a sudden they aren't your customer anymore because of something you did or something you didn't do for them, or for whatever reason. It's disappointing, but you kind of have to say "next" and move on.

Q. Do you handle that differently with friends than strangers?

A. To a certain extent probably. But in general, you have to be tough and say, "We'll miss you, but we're going to move on and have fun without you."

Q. Looking back now, is there anything you wish you had done or done sooner?

A. No, not really. It's a process you just keep working on. Like a friend of mine says, "You just keep doing the same things you've been doing." Hindsight is always good, but you live, learn and move on.

Q. If you had a slogan to live by or something you would put on your tombstone, what would it be?

A. Treat people well I guess. Be nice to people, have empathy and life will be good. You are going to have good and bad things happen, but generally, life is good.

Q. Do you suggest finding a good marketing coach, mentor or mastermind group?

A. All of that stuff is good. If you really want to be the best, then go learn from the best. It's not an end-all, but it is part of the puzzle and process. It depends whether you are going to pay them or they are going to do it for free, along with how much time and involvement is needed. As long as people are willing to teach you and be a mentor when you ask, then yes.

Q. How do you keep your team motivated?

A. That is a good question because our team is huge. We have a lot of people out there. For us it is communication and throwing out ideas and goals. Keeping them focused on the end results. There are a lot of different ways. You try to be as successful as possible.

Q. How has becoming successful at networking changed you?

A. I think probably I am more empathetic, worldlier, and I understand people better. I realize that people aren't perfect; I'm not perfect. I just keep learning.

Q. In a chance meeting, someone asks you what you do, what might you say that takes 30 seconds?

A. "We put people together. We are an introduction service, not an escort service, but an introduction service. We introduce people to other people. People who want to do business with people who want to get business done." That's the main thing. We hook people up.

Q. How important is follow-up to a professional networker or attraction marketer?

A. I think it's critical. If you aren't going to call me back, we can't even talk to get started. I may want to do business with you but I can't give you my business if you don't call me back. If you don't follow-up with people; if you have so much business that you can let a lot of it fall away because you are doing well, then you really aren't making friends by acting that way.

Q. What are the most effective ways you have found to follow up with people?

A. That's a good question. Try to do what is best for the common good and stay in contact with as many peo-

Gene Hamilton

ple as possible with what is most efficient. You can't be calling 100 people every week, or 200, 500 or even 20 people every week. There are a lot of different ways to stay in touch with people. Call people you need to call. Meeting face-to-face is good too, but you can only have so many face-to-face meetings. Talk on the phone to determine if there is a common value. Email as well.

Q. What is your attitude towards competition?

A. It is good as long as it is ethical. We are never in a monopoly situation. Hopefully the competition will be ethical and not pull any stunts. I don't think it is necessary to put the competition down. It is important to point out the difference between yourself and your competition. If someone is trying to steal business or copy your product and sell it for themselves, that's not very ethical. Everyone coming up with their own ideas is good.

Q. Is competition always really competition or can it sometime be a joint venture opportunity if you can be creative?

A. I think it can always be a joint venture, but I don't see this happen in a lot of cases. People say, "Oh, we're in competition, I don't want to work with you." But, I've seen two health insurance agents come to a meeting and one of them wound up going to work for the other one. If you think about it in terms of "We're competition, therefore we're enemies," then that's not a good situation. You can still sit there and be nice to each other. Who knows what could happen from that. They may be able to pass business back and forth. You never really know until they talk.

Q. If I had 15 to 30 minutes a day to devote to improving my networking and attractive marketing skills, what would you recommend I do with that time?

A. You can do a lot of things. I would maybe read. Or, do a Google search to look at different networks and see what each is doing. Stay up with your competition and stay up with other people's ideas because this does not take a long time. Doing this daily is effective, it can add up over a long period of time, and be very rewarding.

Q. **Is there anything else you want to share with an aspiring networker?**
A. Keep it up. Really, the only way to fail is to stop doing it. I hear a lot of network marketing companies say that. It's not always true, but if it's not really for you, then you want to find something that is a better fit.

But, I think it is true from the standpoint that yes, people quit networking because they think it's going to be easy. They get into it and realize it's going to be a lot harder than they thought. Building leads groups and networking is very hard work, but it's also very rewarding.

Most things in life that are of value are not easy. People want a quick scheme, but these don't exist. Typically, success comes because a person put in a lot hard work and consistency. And, don't quit too soon. People often quit right before they get successful. Before you quit, be definitely sure that "Yes, this is something I do not want to do anymore and I want to quit." Otherwise be persistent and you'll be successful.

Q. **How do you maintain a perspective that serves you in these tough times? You hear other businesses sharing their stories of woe in the economy.**
A. It's a tough time out there, and I think it's going to get better. But, it seems like sometimes it gets worse before it gets better. People are dropping out all over

Gene Hamilton

the place. Just stay positive. I'd really hang out with positive people. It's what you put in your head. You have to be very cautious of who you are listening to because if they are gloom and doom, you are putting gloom and doom in your head. If you are hanging out with positive people and listening to positive messages, then you are putting positive things in your head. This is very important.

Q. What do you see as the most common trap your peers fall into? Think back to your colleagues that no longer have businesses. Can you recall what caused their demise?

A. Probably it is thinking that this is a get rich quick thing. Thinking that they can make a homerun, or shoot the elephant, take one shot and boom, they are there! They are not constantly moving in the same direction all the time, gaining the slight edge. If you are doing the right things you'll get there. If you aren't doing the right things, it's not like eating the hamburger and dying of a heart attack immediately. However, if you eat a big greasy hamburger two times a day for a while, it's going to cause health problems eventually. It's a slight edge: either you are doing the right things consistently over time and you get better. Or, you are doing the wrong things consistently over time and you get worse. You always want to be on the slight edge of moving up and doing better.

Q. What do you see as some of the biggest opportunities for new networkers? Any fields that raise red flags or should be avoided?

A. If you are doing something just because you are going to get rich out of it, it's not a good thing. It has to be something you really enjoy doing. Get better at it, and the money will follow. If you are not really enjoying it, even if you are making money, you stop doing it.

Summary

- Have a genuine interest in someone. This is attractive!
- People want to be treated with honesty, integrity and a caring attitude
- Treat people well. Be nice to people, have empathy, and life is good
- Hang out with positive people
- It's not the person that gets the most leads or business cards that wins; it's the person who creates the most meaningful relationships
- The big thing with leads groups is "give to get", and it is not a one to one ratio
- It is good to hear people speak multiple times because you might pick up something new that you can utilize later to help them, or others, out
- If you really want to be the best, then go learn from the best
- There are disappointments. Say "next" and move on
- People want a quick scheme, but these don't exist
- Find something you really enjoy doing, get better at it, and the money will follow
- Doing the right things consistently over time, you get better; doing the wrong things consistently over time, you get worse
- Follow-up is critical

Gene Hamilton's recommended resources

- *The Referral of a Lifetime* – Tim Templeton
- *Endless Referrals* – Bob Burg

Gene Hamilton's recommended resources online

http://50networkers.com/gene-hamilton

Gene Hamilton

FIVE

K eep pushing yourself to be a better
person; don't stop!
Rob McNealy,
U.S. Congressional Candidate

Rob McNealy was the first U.S. Congressional candidate to announce his race for office via Twitter. He is running for the 6th Congressional District in his home state of Colorado. An entrepreneur with multiple businesses, Rob has a strong understanding of networking, both online and offline, and of the value of building and maintaining quality relationships for long term mutual benefit. Rob currently has three businesses in various lifecycle stages. An MBA graduate from Colorado State University, he has been "The Floor Guy" for many years. One of his companies, Contrived Media, which he founded in 2007 does social media consulting and his most recent business venture is a startup called Atlas Medical Devices.

Rob's wife Kristie is a medically trained blogger at KristieMcNealy.com. Rob is extremely well connected with people that he has helped over the years. A quick online search will find him all over the Internet in places like RobMcNealy.com, ContrivedMedia.com, and AskAFloorGuy.com or on Twitter @RobMcNealy. Rob is a living example of the need for good interpersonal and networking skills for whatever field you are in, whether you are "just

ROB McNEALY

a floor guy" or a candidate for United States public office.

"To me, the race has a lot of obstacles and hurdles with someone of my background who has never been a politician or run for office before. However, the great parts are the amazing people that I am meeting and the things that I am learning about marketing in politics. They are things I will use the rest of my life. Regardless of the outcome of this race, the things that I am gaining just for doing this such as running a campaign and running for office are amazing!"

Q. When you started networking, how long did it take you to see tangible results?

A. For in person networking I would say probably about a year. In the first year I learned those things just kind of on my own. I didn't have the advantage of a mentor or any classes on it. I was scared to death when I first started going to my first networking event which I thought was a high-class networking event, and it took me some time. I had an ego thing because I was running a construction company and I had an MBA. All these people I was going to networking events with were business people with their suits and I am just "Mr. Floor Guy". Then after a while I got over the ego saying, "You know what? I am taking care of my family. I don't have a boss. I am making good money and I am utilizing skills I learned at business school." Later I found out that I was making more money than most of the people that I was going to these networking events

> *"Running for office? It's another marketing project. The most enormous, gargantuan marketing project I have ever undertaken."*

with and that made it a lot easier to deal with. Now I say that I'm just a floor guy and that's fine.

Q. How long before you started to see tangible results with people giving you referrals?

A. Oh, immediately. I would say within about three to six months of networking I started understanding the players, the hierarchy – the social business hierarchy – in Colorado. I think the most important thing you can learn about networking is every time you go somewhere ask for another referral. Think of it as a viral thing. What I always try to do when I network with people is when I meet someone – I say, "How can I help this person?" This is probably the most important thing you can do in your networking. For a lot of people something that's hard is reading people or being able to read people's body language and gestures and trying to sort out what they need or what they want.

I don't like the word altruistic – but I like going into networking and looking at it as what I call "The triple win." How you can benefit, how they can benefit, and how the other people you might be doing business with can benefit.

It's a very selfish reason: for one, I want to look like the good guy. Two, it's nice to have a lot of people owing you one, and I can tell you now that I am going into office, I am calling in a lot of those IOU's right now and I am getting them answered. I would have no chance of being elected or having any kind of infrastructure at all If I had not built up a network over the last four or five years. People who I have helped over the last five years are all saying, "Hey, let me know how I can help you, Rob," when I announced that I was doing this.

I believe in the concept of social promotion or maybe

Rob McNealy

political promotion; networking is like a ladder and ultimately you climb rung to rung. When you are starting out, you are at the bottom of that rung. You don't know anybody and typically this is why a lot of people who are unemployed are all of a sudden, "Well, I just got unemployed, now I've got to go network so I can get a job." Well that's great, but it's going to take you at least a year, year and a half, to build a network that can get you a job. People should always be networking; I don't care if they are an employer, an employee or a politician; they should always be building relationships the entire time because that's where the true value is.

> *"...depending on what you are doing in person, you can see results pretty fast. Most of the time, just get off your butt and go somewhere and talk to somebody."*

When you are networking, it takes social skills. So if you are a social person, if you are an extrovert, if you are interesting, those are the things that are going to make you more successful. If those social skills and those social instincts to be able to read people and build rapport are not innate, are not something you are comfortable with, that's going to set you back maybe a year.

You need to recognize that some people have this awkwardness – some people don't even realize that they have it. They just don't understand why they are bad at networking. Some of those people might need a coach to get them past that. I think, depending on what you are doing in person, you can see results pretty fast. Most of the time, just get off your butt and go somewhere and talk to somebody.

I am happy if I go to an event and I make one good connection. If you think about it, one is a number; everything in this world is a numbers game regardless of the people that say it's not about numbers. It absolutely is about numbers. The more people you know that like you and the more people that you have helped, the farther you are going to get in life. Bottom line!

Same thing with online networking and social networking: the more people that can see you, the better off you are. Let me ask you a question – Is it better to have more people reading your blog or less people reading your blog? If you are writing a book, do you want more people to read that book or less people to read that book? I am on Twitter; do I want more people to read my tweets or less people to read my tweets? More! It's the same concept – if you are a television star, if you are a movie actor, is it better that more people see these things or less or fewer? Obviously more, so I apply that approach.

I am not a fan of speed networking concepts. If you go to one networking event a month, in a long night, you might have five interesting conversations if you are trying to sincerely get to know people. In my experience, of those five conversations, you will typically end up with one good connection that could help you somewhere or that you could help and maybe have an IOU come back to you down the line.

So if you go to one networking event a month over the course of a year, you might have twelve good connections. Twelve people that you might like that you might be friends with; that might be able to help you get a job, or help you with your business, or introduce you to somebody else. They may not be able to help you in any way, but they might know somebody that

ROB McNEALY

could really help you. What if you go to five network-ing events a month? Statistically over the course of the year you might have 60 good connections. Do you think it would be better to have 12 good connections of people that can help you and you can help, or 60?

I always make a good connection somewhere, almost every time! I know I am going to go out. I am going to meet somebody that's cool, or somebody that I can have a good conversation with, or someone that can just be a friend. That's how I view networking; I am trying to make friends, and friends help each other. But I would rather have more friends than fewer friends along the way.

I go to these events and get people I can develop rela-tionships with over time. You can't just go to one event and expect someone to hire you or be a client or what-ever. It just doesn't work like that.

For instance, there is this thing I do called "Taste Cast-ing," which is where restaurants will give us free food and a group of social media people will all come out, take pictures, blog about how great the restaurant is, or if they don't like it – say it's not that great. It is kind of like an exchange for food, critics for marketing. I had no clue that one guy's wife even worked in spinal implants. He is one of the organizers. I took them both out to dinner and over the course of a two and a half hour meal, I learned the exact sales process on how the sales reps typically succeed in getting in to see the doctor

> *"...develop relationships with over time. You can't just go to one event and ex-pect someone to hire you or be a client or whatever. It just doesn't work like that."*

that she worked for. You never know where a strategic relationship that you make now may help you in a year or two.

Q. The "Taste Casting" thing: Has that been affected at all by the new FTC ruling that came in that says that if you get any kind of monetary or gifting for a review, you've got to declare it?

Author's Note: Rob is not a lawyer, so this comment should be understood as his personal opinion, not as legal advice.

A. You know it's interesting. I am sure the regulations apply to it. The problem is that I don't like those laws for a variety of reasons because I don't think social media people should be held to a higher standard than radio and television. This treats them – treats social media – at a higher standard.

I can name you two television shows here in Denver right now that are on during the day where they bring people on to talk about something and I know for a fact that they paid to be on there. You can't get on those shows without paying. They don't disclaim that, or acknowledge it anywhere, that the people and guests are paying.

If you think about it, maybe it's not technically an endorsement, but when you invite someone on a show and interview them, it is a passive endorsement. If people know that they paid to be on there and it's just a paid review, that's not as credible as if people think it is news. When you are invited, the concept of truth agents or trust agents come into play. People think, at least subconsciously – if you are on radio or television, you must be doing something right, you must be an expert or really credible, and they are not disclosing that these people are paying to be there. I would argue that that is a passive endorsement.

That's what I don't like about it. It is not being applied across the board. Where this came from is in the affiliate marketing industry, there are people that were making fake reviews on websites, deliberately – on blogs and things like that – and there were people that were just out right lying and getting paid. They had never even seen the product. Ultimately, I think that's a bit disingenuous, but there are a lot of people that are in a grey area that are going to be affected by this. For instance, there are bloggers out there that do review sites and I have one of these sites myself. I talk about a product and then I have a referral link where someone can buy the product.

If I just say how great the product is and it's got all these features, but yet I am not being paid for that unless you buy, ultimately that's a grey area – because I am not saying it's the best product in the world, but just writing about the product, its features, and what it does, based on manufacturers information and providing a link to where people can buy it and if they buy it I get a referral fee, a commission. That's kind of that grey area because technically, do you have the product? Are you really using it? No, obviously not, but on the other side of it, I don't know anybody on the radio who endorses these products and has ever tried them either. I've worked in radio and it doesn't happen. They just get paid to endorse and discuss.

So, that's what I don't like – the fact that radio and television are not being held to the same standard. I believe a lot of this came out from the lobbying from the radio and television industry because they are losing out market share and eyeballs to new media and social media, and they wanted to level the playing field in their favor; unlevel the playing field in their favor is what happened. It hurts a lot of people that are like me who are now all of a sudden doing something that is grey-hat which didn't use to be grey-hat. I'm just writing a site talking about products and features and then I link to it. Actually the best way to sell something is to talk about it.

There are some people who cross the line, who outright lie and say, "Hey, I have been using this product for ten years and I have lost 50 pounds," and they never even looked at the product. That's the problem. You have a lot of people that are doing bad stuff; that's where the FTC ruling came out of. So, I understand why that is – because that's fraud, but there are a lot of people who aren't doing fraud that are now affected. It's like a couple bad apples spoiled the bunch in this case.

Q. **A lot is said about having a catchy, 30-second elevator speech that you can deliver confidently in a networking situation. How important do you think that is?**

A. Well, I think it's important. You need to be able to articulate who you are and most importantly I think the bigger part of that is not the speech, but the confidence. You need to be confident with what you do and who you are. I would say as boring as this is, one of the first things people say is, "So what do you do for a living?" I don't ever have the same answer, but I am confident when I say it.

I will give a different elevator pitch depending on what I am doing. So, I am not going to give the floor pitch if I am over at a spinal implant conference, and if I am at a political thing – it just changes. I think you need to be able to be a little chameleon like and you need to sound confident. Think of a sound bite; come up with your own sound bite. So, for a political speech, I might give something like this; "Hey, I am Rob McNealy, I am a serial entrepreneur. I hail from Metro Detroit. I worked my way through school. I have this great new project I am working on. I am running for office. I am a libertarian. I know third parties don't typically get taken seriously, but I am the guy to watch and you need to take me seriously. Most people are libertarian and don't know it. The question is: What's a libertarian? A libertarian is someone who is fiscally responsible and socially tolerant. Most people fall under that category.

Most people don't want the government to take more from them and most people want what the government takes from them to be spent in a sustainable and frugal and responsible manner. Most people just don't want the government to tell them how to live their lives. That's what a libertarian is." More importantly you need to be able to clearly articulate, know when to shut it off, and be confident with it. That's the most important thing.

There are a lot of laid off people looking for jobs, right? And these people are like the piranha of networking events because they reek with desperation. It is typical because they don't know how to network because they never had to. Most employees other than sales guys don't network. The CEO's and the sales guys are the networkers; most the others are just waiting to get the hell out at 5:00 and go home. If you think about it, most employees don't want to think about work when they are at home. They don't want to take their weekend time to go to networking events, especially if they don't get paid for it.

So, all of a sudden, when the networking skills should be the most honed – when they are looking for a job

– that is when they are the least honed because they are not used to networking at all. You can smell these guys; they are timid, they don't know how to do small talk, they are not very interesting because they are not doing a whole lot of interesting things. They are just looking for a job and they are just like, "I am in transition!" That's great; why don't you say, "I got laid off and I am looking for work," because to guys like me, that would be a lot more truthful than trying to use big buzz words. Ultimately, to answer your question, I think confidence is the most important piece to that. It doesn't matter what you say; keep it interesting and be confident.

Q. Actually, there is a follow on to that: What makes the difference between an attractive networker, a boring networker, and an irritating networker?

A. I think most people want to be entertained, across the board. You know, who is the person at the party that is getting all the attention? It's the guy that makes people laugh. It's not the guy who sits and grumbles, "I hate the government and corporation took advantage of me," and blah blah. You don't want to talk to that guy! He's annoying; he's a downer! It doesn't matter what the guy says, it matters how they come off.

If you come off interesting and you can tell good stories, that's where you become interesting. That's what makes you memorable, ultimately. So, I don't know… I have done a lot of crazy stuff in my days. The good thing is I have had a lot of experiences from working in a lot of different companies in corporate because I never lasted very long in any one company. I am too ADHD and I didn't realize I was an entrepreneur. When you are an entrepreneur trying to be a corporate guy, that doesn't usually mix. You burn out, you get pissy and frustrated. I had a lot of experience working

ROB MCNEALY

for different industries because I bounced around a lot which has actually been a great source of experience for me because I have been able to talk about things. I have worked in the automotive industry in Detroit. I have worked for a Japanese company. I have worked for a Swiss company. I have traveled around Europe. I have lived in a foreign country.

Now I have kids. You can pull from all these different experiences and you can come up with interesting stories that other people might not have had. So, generally, you find out where the common ground is and then you start tapping into interesting anecdotes. Be interesting, and funny, bottom line. But don't be timid and don't be nervous because people will detect that and they will want to run from you. If I am looking for a guy and one says, "I am in transition, I am struggling..." The whole time, the guy is talking to you like you are his bartender or psychiatrist or counselor. Rather than whining about all the bad things that happened to you, why don't you tell me the good things? Okay, the world sucks, so tell me good things. What do you want to do? Where do you want to go?

I am pretty accommodating to people who go to a networking party and are in transition because it's a tough time for them, but ultimately, when people are desperate – and I understand that their world is collapsing – what they are trying to do is all about them at that point. Not about you. So a lot of in-transition, desperate people come off as very selfish because it's about them rather than about trying to foster a relationship and learn something about the other person, which ultimately is the most fundamentally important part about networking.

Q. Okay, so it is vitally important to be interesting and

to entertain, but it's also important not to be so caught up in yourself with trying to be interesting that you actually can show an interest in the other person.

A. Yes, and I struggle with that because I have a big mouth. Around some people, I can be domineering. If someone doesn't shut me up sometimes, and I get really keyed up about something, I'll dominate. I know that's one of my own flaws and I continue to work on that. That's why I keep telling you if I just keep rambling, cut me down.

Q. **What things have you done consciously to try to improve your networking skills?**

A. Well, when I first started out, I read some books. I did the self-help kind of route and I asked people who are networkers how they did it, and I watched how people did it. That's where I started trying to figure out who were the successful networkers. I also looked at myself and tried to be objective and see why things went real well for some people I networked with and then why it didn't with others. I found – when I immediately try to find out how can you help me, me, me? That turned people off, but when I went into it with, "How can I help you first?" and fired the first shot over the bow – "Hey, how can I hook you up?" That seemed to go over better. So, I just kind of looked at what worked and what didn't.

Q. **What do you think is more important: your confidence in your skills, your personality, your posture, or actually being able to provide real value to people?**

A. Ultimately, you have to provide value, and if you don't have the value you find the value because ultimately your credibility will be ruined if you don't. Simple as that! Let me give you an example: I know a lot of people who are really, really good talkers; they really

ROB McNEALY

talk a good game like they know what they are talking about, and a lot of people are baffled by their BS, but when the rubber meets the road, they can't deliver. I have met a lot of people like that, so I think ultimately the most important thing is you need to provide the value that you say you can.

Don't ever over-promise something or promise to deliver something you won't or can't. In the long term it will kill you. I know there are a lot of guys in the small business community out here that are considered laughing stocks. People are like, "Oh! You got stuck in a meeting with that guy?" because they are just full of crap and they don't deliver.

Q. **If I was just starting out with a brand new company, or as a new associate, or as an employee of an established company, what would be the best use of my time initially to start developing my networking skills?**

A. For someone who has very little experience with their work – build a board of advisors. Those are the first people you network with. This is something I did with my night vision company at the end when I should have done it at the beginning. It cost me a couple hundred thousand dollars not to do it this way. Get your board of advisors on board, offer to pay them, write up a memo of understanding stating that you will pay them $100 an hour and you only need them a couple of hours a quarter, and it could just be on the phone if they are not in the same state as you. That's what I would recommend and about the most priceless piece of advice that I wish someone had given to me.

Q. **Okay, so online networking, offline networking – do you find one better than the other? Is it just a matter of personal style and skills?**

A. My own personal style which I have come to believe over the last couple of years is that in-person networking is local; it's going to be deeper and tend to be a narrower niche. You are going to develop much better interpersonal skills with in-person networking. Online networking tends to be much shallower, but much wider across the board. They both have their purposes. I don't think one replaces the other; I think they complement each other.

Online marketing gives you two things: One: It's not as rich to network online, it takes longer to build rapport online, but you can build relationships with people in different states or countries in real time which you may never have met just trying to do local networking. Two: with tools, you can build a following or a network – There is a much bigger economy of scale with online networking than with in-person networking.

Q. **Do you find social media to be a distraction or a benefit in networking your business?**

A. For some people. I think it just comes down to discipline, work practices, best practices, and practice. I weave social media into checking Twitter, Facebook messages, tweet, direct messages, and email are all the same thing to me. They are all just part of my work flow.

Q. **Sometimes it can seem overwhelming with so many new things to learn and think about as you are just getting started. Are people generally fairly forgiving as a new networker stumbles through the learning process?**

A. If people are aware of it, sure. Some people aren't, but those people are jerks anyways. There's always going to be jerks. It just depends on what you do. If you are genuinely being sincere and someone is a jerk to you, well they are going to be a jerk no matter what so don't worry about it.

Q. Are there any particular unforgiveable mistakes that a new networker should take extra care to avoid?

A. Well, for interpersonal relationships – and I am a hypocrite on this – but stay away from religion and politics. I am in politics, so that's my thing. When you are around people you don't know, you don't know where they are coming from so it is never a good idea to start spouting off a strong opinion about one thing or another. I have seen a lot of people make that mistake and I know I certainly have.

Q. Do you ever feel overwhelmed with the sheer amount of things that you know you have to learn or improve to achieve the success you desire?

A. You've just got to keep trucking, man. I realize that I will always be learning the rest of my life. It never ends, so don't try to race to the finish line because the finish line is always moving. Just know that you are on the track and that you are going in the right direction.

Q. How important is it to be clear on your personal and business core values in relating to people in a networking context?

A. I would say that that is pretty straight forward. Don't be a jerk, don't be a thief; don't be a fraud, don't be a liar. There are people who get through life doing that. If that's your short term view it's about churn and burn. I don't respect that and I don't think it is sustainable. If you can't make a living, yet you claim to have a million dollars in the bank and that you're driving your beater car and then you tell people it's your son's car because your car is in the shop – I know people that have made up whoppers like this – and I am like,

"Don't lie to me." I ultimately think that those people are missing out on great long-term friendships and opportunities and I just don't think it is very sustainable. It is bordering on illegal.

Relationships are built on trust, common interest, and mutual admiration and respect. If you are taking away the parts of that, you are never going to build a real relationship and then you are not going to get the long-term benefit of it. I would just say that you've got to be a nice person. Stick to your values; why lie?

Q. How do you attract quality people into your network, who might be good power partners, peer advisors or joint venture partners? People you can trust your referrals to or people who might refer others to you?

A. Think of it as dating. You just didn't meet your wife last week and then get married this week. You got to know her. Well, would you refer your wife to somebody? Of course you would. You would give a referral to your wife because you trust her, you know her, you married her, you love her, and you must have respect for her.

I think it just takes time. Some people you develop a rapport with, you get to know their core being and their principles and you see them live those principles time and time again in different circumstances and different situations, and you trust that and then you refer them. If you only see a person once every six months and you don't have a lot of good experiences being outside a controlled networking environment, well you have no idea.

Ultimately, if you refer someone and they screw up, it looks badly on you. Don't give a referral for someone you don't know and don't trust adequately. It will

Rob McNealy

hurt you long term if they screw up, or steal, or blow up, or whatever they do.

Q. Does letting go of any emotional expectation of a sale, or your own personal agenda from a networking interaction, free you to have a more successful interaction?

A. Because you are focusing on their needs and not your own, you are going to come off more sincere and you might be able to build a better, thicker bond just from the fact that you are trying to help them. If you come off sincerely trying to help them in some way, it will come back, but I think you should have zero expectation of anything coming back to you because then you won't be disappointed if it doesn't and some people don't reciprocate. You never know; it's a crap-shoot. You are making investments in time and relationships. Some become really fruitful and some not so much.

Q. How important is advertising to your business? Do you think that advertising or networking is a better use of your time and resources or is it important to do both?

A. Both. And different businesses are going to be marketed differently. In fact, for my flooring company, I do very little networking now. It's almost all advertising whereas with my new business, it is going to be almost no advertising and pretty much all networking relationship building on my sales reps part. It's just a different industry; things are done differently based on industry, at least in my experience. I would say try to find someone who is there doing it already and pick their brain. Find out how it's done, who the gatekeepers are, what are the expected norms in the industry, so you don't go in there and blow a couple sales before you realize, "Oh, I shouldn't have done that; that's not how it is done." Incentivize those people; take them

U.S. CONGRESSIONAL CANDIDATE

out to dinner; take them out for a couple beers; be nice to them.

Q. **Do you think that luck and timing have a lot to do with success in networking or attraction marketing? Or are there one or two other factors which have played a big part for you?**

A. I don't know about luck; I think the more you show up the more you are going to run into people who can help you versus if you are not out there then you have no chance.

Q. **Is there anything you wish you had known or done sooner?**

A. The advisory board for a specific business. How to network in general? I wish somebody would have told me this when I was 18. I could have saved ten years of my life or been further along economically – ten years further ahead – had I had a really good mentor or a series of mentors. I wish I had developed people skills much earlier in life and those things could have been taught to me. I was willing and open; I just wasn't in the place at that time. I didn't know where to start. Hindsight is always 20/20.

Q. **Is there anything else you would want to share with an aspiring networker or attraction marketer?**

A. I think the most important thing I could say is I don't like the word networking. I like the words "relationship building," and relationship building networking should be an act that you do your entire life, not for a finite period of time. So don't think, "Oh I got laid off," and then network for six months, find a job, then stop networking. I see this a lot. It almost seems disingenuous. Again, it goes back to that immediate, it's-all-about-me, me, me, me and guess what? Now that you've got a job and you stopped networking, maybe

Rob McNealy

if you got a job, you could help some of those other people that didn't have a job. Maybe you could just teach them or inspire them on how to do things better on their job search or their networking. Don't just take, take, and take in this world; give back too.

Q. Do you have a particular slogan to live by?

A. Just don't be a jerk; we have too many jerks in this world. We need less of them.

Q. Does simply providing excellent customer service alone help your business to grow by word of mouth or is this just the minimum requirement?

A. Hmm...I never thought of it like that. I would say business grows with crappy customer service, but I think they grow better with excellent customer service, so I always strive for that.

Q. Does providing excellent customer service automatically give you word-of-mouth advertising or do you have to encourage that in some way?

A. Yes, and yes. I think if you do a good job, people are going to talk about it, but if you incentivize and encourage people to talk about that job that you did for them, you are going to get more of that word-of-mouth going.

Q. How important is networking for the political arena?

A. More important than for business. Right or wrong – it's who you know and it's who is going to give you a break and who is going to give you an endorsement and all that kind of networking, absolutely.

Q. Some people look at networking as free advertising, but it's hardly free when in reality there's a cost in time and money to attend various networking events. How has consistency in developing your network

U.S. CONGRESSIONAL CANDIDATE

paid off for you?

A. I would say persistence is everything. You can't stop; you've got to constantly be working at it. As I move further and further along in life, I am always trying to work on my own flaws and weaknesses. It's a constant struggle; you've got to be persistent at working at it and developing relationships and reaching out.

Sometimes networking can be boring; sometimes it is tedious in trying to hook people up. It is time consuming. You are making an investment in yourself and these other people and not all those people are going to repay that investment. You are not going to get an ROI from everybody, but the problem is you never know where it is going to come from or where it is not going to come from.

Q. **What is your attitude towards competition?**

A. I am very supportive of competition. Competition breeds quality, breeds innovation, makes me want to be a better person so I can be more competitive. I think competition as it is applied in most situations is actually a good thing.

Q. **Is competition always competition or if you could be creative could some of your best opportunities for collaboration and joint ventures come out of competition?**

A. I believe that it's interesting to be an entrepreneur; even my competitors are collaborative because we are willing to help the industry or want to help ourselves. It seems like when I was in the corporate world it was a very competitive in a negative way meaning that it was a churn and burn kind of competition. Meaning that I had to step on somebody else's head to get to where I wanted to be. Whereas entrepreneurs are like, "I will help you out; no big deal." Like the affiliate

Rob McNealy

marketing industry which is online marketers, they tend to be some of the most collaborative bunches out there in the planet. They might not give all their cards away, but they are more than happy to help you with what you are doing. I think you have to have a collaborative attitude, but I think competition is a great thing too.

Q. **How do you keep your team motivated? When I say "team," you've obviously got a team of people helping you with running for office when you are in your entrepreneurial ventures, you have team there. How do you keep them motivated over time?**

A. I am used to incentivizing people's behaviors. I think for anything, first and foremost is you have to screen and attract the right people on the team to begin with, people who are vested and inspired with you and your causes – no matter what it is. With the campaign, I am trying to find people that believe in what I am doing and convincing them and persuading them that I think I have a chance. I then explain to them the strategy that I have to make what I say happen, and then ultimately I am saying that I want them to win too.

I always look for how I can help them, even if the ratio is off. If they have helped me a lot more than I could help them, the fact that I am trying to help them tends to motivate the volunteers and the people that are donating their time and money. They at least know that I appreciate what they are doing and am not just trying to take advantage of it.

On the business side of it, you've got to find the right people that are passionate that are really working toward a goal, then you look at finding out what their internal self-development and personal goals are. When you are determining whether you are going to hire

U.S. CONGRESSIONAL CANDIDATE

them, try to figure out "With the goals of my company – if they grow with my company, what kind of investment can I make in them and their personal goals?" I then see if I can align the strategy of hiring them with enhancing their personal development as well.

Q. Do you have any particular recommended training resources, books, classes, anything like that which just comes to mind?

A. *Unfair Advantage*. That is an NLP book that I read and liked. *Think and Grow Rich* and *Rich Dad, Poor Dad* have a good mind set. Also, any book written by Dan Pink.

Q. How important is follow-up to a professional networker or attraction marketer?

A. It's vital; most people don't. Straight out of the gate, most people don't ever follow-up. I went to a networking event a week and a half ago. I gave out a bunch of cards and no one followed up, but out of all the people I met – I met like seven people – I have already followed-up. Most of them, I didn't see any real connection there, but I followed-up with two of them.

Q. What are the most effective ways to follow-up that you have found?

A. My typical strategy that has worked for me is that I will go out and I will just invite them to coffee if I feel there was a connection and say, "Hey, I have no agenda; I just wanted to see if you have time to grab coffee." Get to know the person a little deeper, ask them about their family, and find out where they are from. Find some common ground – "Do you like to golf? Do you like to ski? What do you want out of life?" I just email them or call them and invite them out to coffee and see where it goes.

Q. Is there anything in particular that you have found

that doesn't work very well for you for following up?

A. "Hi, I am Rob McNealy. Do you have a customer for me?" That doesn't work.

Q. If I had about 15 to 30 minutes a day to devote to improving my networking and attraction marketing skills, what would you recommend I do with that time?

A. Not including going to events – two minutes for phone calls, 20 minutes for online marketing, and 10 minutes to send emails to invite people to coffee.

Q. What do you see as the most common trap that your peers fall into?

A. They give up, they stop learning, they stop living; Most people don't live up to their potential because they just stop.

Q. All the people you network with and all the time you spend networking, how important is balance in your life?

A. I live a very holistic life. Everything is woven in. For me, there is no clear delineation between work and play, necessarily. For instance, I keep everything on a calendar or I wouldn't keep anything straight, but I blocked off a good chunk of the day for my kid's birthday. That was actually an event on my calendar, so I treat personal time like business time and schedule it and make sure it happens; otherwise I will lose sight. I am a really hard-charging, "Type A" kind of guy, so I am always running at full throttle, mentally at least, and I never stop. My wife is not that way so I have to be cognizant of what her limits are and not try to force my drive onto her. I think you just have to find your balance and limits and try not to go over them too much, but get as close to your limits as you can. Maximize your ability and commitment to it. Just try not to go over that line too often because then you will get burned out.

Summary
- Don't be a jerk. We need less of them
- I don't like the word networking. I like the words "relationship building"
- Aim for the triple win – "How you can benefit, how they can benefit, and how the other people you might be doing business with can benefit"
- Follow-up is vital. Most people don't follow up at all
- Persistence is everything. You can't stop; if you get what you were hoping for through networking, keep networking. You may be able to help someone else through your network
- Learn to give back
- Stay away from religion and politics with people you don't know well, unless religion or politics are your main thing as a professional
- Develop people skills as early as you can in life. Get a mentor or training if you need it
- Most of the time, just get off your butt, go somewhere and talk to somebody

Rob McNealy's recommended resources
- *The Unfair Advantage: Sell with NLP!* by Duane Lakin
- *Think and Grow Rich* by Napoleon Hill
- *Rich Dad, Poor Dad* by Robert Kiyosaki
- Any book written by Dan Pink

Rob McNealy's recommended resources
Online
http://50networkers.com/rob-mcnealy

Rob McNealy

Stop looking for the people that you are looking for, and start looking for the people that are looking for you.

**Jason O'Toole,
Network/Internet
Marketer and Trainer,
Founder of
YourProspex.com**

Jason O'Toole is a successful marketer and trainer. He carved out his niche designing online training programs and marketing systems. Jason founded www.yourpros-pex.com, an online generic training company that teaches people how to build their business both online and offline.

Raised in the small town of Lincoln, New Brunswick, he studied computer science at the University of New Brunswick, and worked in the computer security field for the Canadian government and large consulting firms like Ernst & Young. Having an entrepreneurial spirit from an early age, and a philosophical preference towards working for a profit rather than a wage, Jason, at 25, started his own computer security consulting firm which is still running strong seven years later.

At age 28, Jason discovered another life changing concept – residual and passive income. This was when he was introduced to the network marketing industry, which provided him a venue for sharing his knowledge and passion of entrepreneurialism with people who really wanted to do more in their business lives, being part of their success, and getting paid to do it. Jason now lives in Ottawa, Canada.

Q. How long were you involved in networking or attraction marketing before you actually started to see some tangible results for your business?

A. My first introduction to the network marketing industry was quite successful. Within about seven months I had built quite a sizable organization. At the time, I had a business partner and we opened up the United Kingdom for the company we were working with. We took care of getting our product in, coming up with a marketing plan and bringing the right people in place. Within seven months – and this was when I quickly realized the power of the industry – we had clients in fifteen countries and many hundreds of people promoting our product. This is when I really started to grab hold of what was possible. While I was sleeping, people were working and earning me a paycheck; this was pretty exciting!

I invested my time networking, primarily person to person; picking up the phone and calling people and using more traditional means of network marketing. At that time, there really was no concept of Internet marketing. There was no online venture, so being from a technical and online background, I started developing a few online systems to support my organization. From the beginning, I had always implemented attraction marketing, it was just done offline. Attraction marketing is a philosophy offline as much as it is online. People join people and although I didn't use the

Internet, I still trained my team on the philosophy that people join people. Bringing that mentality online was a real winner.

Q. What were some of the significant growth areas or turning points along the way?

A. Taking ownership of my business, and understanding that I can pick and choose who I work with. I learned how important picking the right people is for my organization. Eventually, I ran into the roadblock of finding enough people to talk to once I got through my warm market and discovered the impact of attrition in network marketing. Developing leadership, opening foreign markets, what things to do and what not to do, were all important things to learn.

Q. What makes the difference between an irritating networker, a boring networker and an attractive networker?

A. It comes down to where you are in the life cycle of the industry. An irritating networker is someone who gets started in the industry, but doesn't understand how it works. They don't understand the longer-term vision of what they are doing and don't have that understanding of why people get started with them in the first place. They are always harassing you with the latest and greatest company or deal. They really offer no value whatsoever, except in their own minds; where they've got a ground-floor business opportunity and they've got to be the "biggest and baddest" and latest and greatest this or that.

Boring marketers are in the middle between irritating and attractive. As people move along in the evolutionary chain of marketing, they move more from an irritating networker to a boring networker. After they become a little bit more educated, they become a little more fearful of the idea of spamming their business opportunity. Boring networkers lose the excitement and passion they had as irritating networkers. As they move more towards boring, they understand that it's about value. They understand that the reason anyone gets involved with them in business is because people see them (or the people they are introducing them to) as someone who can help them get where they want to go. They can help them to achieve their goals, whether financial or lifestyle. Once networkers start to understand that, they pull back from the irritating activities. They then start doing a whole lot of nothing. They post a lot of information, and they try to position themselves as experts in the industry, but they essentially become scared and don't do much of anything. They are trying to position themselves, to show why people should work with them, but they really don't know how to go about it and become sort of stagnant.

The attractive networker is the "Alpha Networker" – or whatever you want to call them – this is the top person who truly gets it, truly understands it, and truly offers value to other people. For me, an attractive networker is somebody who's out for the greater cause of the industry. They are out to make the industry a better place, to help support, assist, and provide value and guidance to anyone willing to learn. The attractive networker is someone who is able to take a person who is either in that boring position, or even an irritating networker, and help them move into the attractive position. They are willing to coach and help anybody in any company.

Attractive networkers are people who understand that people work with them because of the value they offer. An attractive networker is somebody that really gets it, really understands, and is always giving value back to the industry; not just to their own teams or groups, but working to make the industry a better place. Attractive networkers are always making the assumption close. They understand the value they have, and are primarily focused on relationships. They are always developing strong friendships based on mutual respect they have for their prospects. They know the person they are working with will join them at some point, and they simply focus on helping this person achieve their goals.

Q. What kind of things have you consciously done to improve your networking skills?

A. When I first started networking, learning to prospect and talk to people was my focus. Talking to people was difficult. I found that others also had difficulty prospecting people, because in our minds we knew the only reason we were talking to someone new, was to identify if this person was someone that we would want in our business. I think everybody goes through this struggle at first.

One of the things that I did to become a better networker was to simply talk to people with no ulterior motive or agenda whatsoever. I was just out there meeting individuals, shaking hands, saying, "Hi; how are you," and really finding out about this person. I became good at just making friends with people in a matter of a couple of minutes, and developing that *know* and *like* aspect of the know, like, and trust model. Doing this with a perfect stranger was something that I really worked on very diligently when I first got started in the industry.

Something that I was doing very consciously on the Internet, was always trying to give tips and advice to people that weren't necessarily on my team or orga-

JASON O'TOOLE

nization. That's how my whole system and *Prospex* community came to be through a conscious decision to make a difference in the industry and bring together the best of the best; training minds to give back to the industry as a whole.

Q. What are some training resources you would recommend?

A. For my own attraction-marketing model, it was things that I learned along the way from many individuals. From this I formulated my best approaches and material. I obviously highly recommend my *www.yourprospex.com* free online training model. From my personal networking standpoint, what took my business to the next level and developed my passion for sticking with the industry, was a fellow industry trainer, Tim Sales. Rob Hamilton, one of my best friends to this day, was a stranger to me at the time. He and I purchased Tim's training series. Now five years later, and as friends, Rob and I are building an empire and have launched the Canadian market together.

Tim's DVD training resource, *Brilliant Compensation* has had a huge impact on me. I have easily watched the DVD more than fifty times to the point where I was doing Tim's training for my teams and my groups practically verbatim for what he was teaching us. I highly recommend *Brilliant Compensation*.

Q. Are there any particular "unforgivable" mistakes people make in networking?

A. For people that are just starting out in the industry, I don't know if there is really anything you can do that is unforgivable. Obviously, if you are talking to your immediate family or friends and you are constantly harassing them to the point where they are scared and walk the other way when they see you coming, then you've crossed the line. As someone who is moving towards the professionalism of an attractive marketer, you are going to need to recognize what you are doing. You'll need to pull back, take a couple of deep breaths, and realize that your family and friends aren't the only people out there that you can prospect for your business. Stop working out of desperation because that's what you are doing when you are always chasing your family and friends. Learn the skill set needed to break out of that mindset, and develop the mindset needed to meet more people both online and offline. Of course you should talk to your friends and family; just don't be "that guy".

For people experienced in attraction marketing, the biggest mistake you can possibly make is switching companies and recruiting sidelines (other people in the company who are not on your team) from the company perspective. I have had experiences where the person that I joined in my up-line actually left, went to another company, and recruited my team out from underneath me. Then, this person tried to use my own team as leverage for me to join another opportunity! I think this is probably one of the biggest taboo or unforgivable things that you can do. After saying this, I do believe your response to this person should be based on whether you believe they can grow as a person from this mistake. Giving people a second chance shows you understand how to value people in the networking arena.

Q. **Online and offline networking? Is one better than the other? Do you need both or is it just a matter of personal style and skills?**

A. It truly is about personal style and skills. I am a believer that you do need both. The online method, to me, is a lead generation strategy. If you want to develop a long-term, stable organization; one that is going to pay you for years and years to come, you absolutely, 100%, require that offline skill in the sense of developing leadership, friendship and long lasting relationships. This is really the glue that is going to hold your organization together."

There are two sides to the coin: there's the online and offline with regards to prospecting and identifying new people to talk to about your business, and then there's the aspect of developing your long-term, stable income. When it comes to developing the long-term aspect of your organization, then you absolutely require that offline component in which you are going to have to pick up the phone. You are going to have to do some recognition trips, incentive programs, and things of that sort, to really put the glue together in your organization. You do need both. You are going to want to do the odd meeting where everybody gets together and puts faces to names, and really develops a sense of team spirit; and conference calls, if you are building in foreign markets, things of that sort.

When it comes to lead generation and attraction marketing, it really comes down to personal preference. I do a lot of my stuff online. I generate lots and lots of leads on the Internet and I funnel those leads through my attraction marketing system. I funnel those people

> *"There's no better way to develop your people skills than taking that offline approach; learning how to effectively talk to people and develop relationships very quickly."*

directly to wanting to work with me by offering them value. You can do it this way. I am also very good at just going out there and meeting people. I love meeting people. I

YOURPROSPEX.COM

think you definitely want a blend of both. If you are going to be a network marketer for the long term, you are going to want to develop your leadership and people skills. There's no better way to develop your people skills than taking that offline approach; learning how to effectively talk to people and develop relationships very quickly.

Q. **How do you attract quality people into your network who might be good power partners, peer advisors or joint venture partners? People you can trust your referrals to, or people who might refer others to you?**

A. Great question, Rob. When it comes to developing and expanding your network, these are things I do all the time. You are exactly right – it's not just in network marketing. It is in expanding your core upper echelon level of business partners and friends. For myself, I have always been a huge believer in always giving more than you ever expect in return. If you maintain that philosophy, everything will work itself out. I am also a firm believer in the law of attraction. I believe that if you are always giving, always giving, always giving, you are going to get something in return. And if you don't – hey that's ok too. It's not why you do it to begin with. If you do something for someone only to expect something in return, you've got a self-serving attitude and you need to be more about abundance.

As for identifying as to whether or not I trust a person, this comes down to a personal matter. How well do you know the person? Where did the referral come from? I am all about just helping other people. I have done events here in Ottawa where they are completely outside of network marketing.

I am working on something right now with some local charities. I have been working on something else with

Jason O'Toole

some other entrepreneurs that are looking to develop their online community and do training in the world of entrepreneurialism. I help them to the best of my capabilities and expect nothing in return. So I put 30 or 40 people in a room for one lady's book launch.

We are doing another book launch that I will be promoting, and helping this person put people in a room here in Ottawa. I guess I am not expecting anything back, and I think doing this helps you develop and solidify relationships with people who have the ability to reciprocate if they see a need or feel they can offer value to your network.

I think it's just about helping, helping, helping, always asking people what you can do for them, and not always necessarily looking for a reason to do something for them just because you know that in turn they are going to help you. I think if you've got that self-serving philosophy, you are really going to be limiting yourself from people that could add value to your life. Whether its months, or maybe even years, down the road.

Q. Does letting go of any emotional expectation of a sale, or personal agenda from a networking interaction, free you to have a more successful interaction?

A. Absolutely! I firmly believe this. Often people get started in the industry and have an emotional tie to their product and business. They feel so passionate about it and it really frustrates them to be shut down by friends or prospects. They then become paralyzed with respect to talking about it anymore because they take the rejection personally. They let the decisions and emotions of others impact the way they feel. Don't give people the power to control how you feel about something. Make your own conscious decision about how you feel about it and if you are passionate and excited about it, then run with it.

Often when people say no, it has nothing to do with you; absolutely nothing to do with you. They just don't feel like it. Maybe it's the wrong time for them, or maybe they just don't like that particular thing. You are just the messenger. As you are sharing your message and passion with as many people as you can – some people will get excited about it and they will, in turn, run with you. Others will not. Whatever your process is for putting people through your system, master that process without any emotional outcome as to the end of that process. You just have to get good at putting people through your system. Get good at the process.

Q. What have been the biggest rewards for you from your networking activities?

A. One of the biggest rewards is watching and helping other people achieve their goals. At a convention, I experienced one of my best friends fulfilling his dream – standing up on stage in front of an audience of thousands telling his story – and watching how nervous he was from pure excitement and passion. This is something he has wanted to do his whole life and watching him get a standing ovation halfway through his speech and then another one at the end was one of the most powerful feelings I have experienced in helping somebody achieve a goal.

Another reward is helping people achieve their financial goals. Just in the past five months, we have helped thirty-two people get free BMW cars, and helped hundreds of people earn life-changing income. Seeing the smiles on their faces, seeing them develop the ability to quit their second jobs and spend more time with their families. Things like that are the biggest rewards and biggest driving forces for me, Rob.

Q. What have been your biggest challenges?

A. Developing leaders! I have only recently begun to learn how to master this task. I have been able to attract leaders and have many leaders. But taking somebody who is not a leader, and does not have those qualities and characteristics yet, and developing them into a leader is a huge challenge.

> *"Become the person you wish to recruit and stop trying to recruit the person you're trying to become."*

I have focused on essentially duplicating myself whole-heartedly by enabling people, giving them the tools that they need, and letting them run with their skills. I have learned to stop wanting greater leadership progress in them more than they want it for themselves. To sum it up, really it's about two things: identifying people who want it and will take action at all costs to get it vs. people who merely want it; this is the biggest challenge. The other challenge is teaching people how to become the person they wish to recruit as opposed to recruiting the person they want to be.

Q. How important are "direct response" marketing skills to attraction marketing or networking professionally? Are they complementary, necessary, or something completely different?

A. It is something different and not required. However, at the same time, you will see a massive influx of success from direct response marketing if your system is set up properly to brand yourself on an ongoing basis and not just from the initial response.

You do not require direct-sales marketing. In my online community at yourprospex.com, we teach people first and foremost how to succeed with social media. Most of our training is derived around offering value-based information to individuals who in turn see you as someone who is helping them; someone who sees you as constantly offering value in the community and in the industry as a whole. So, through social marketing, you can essentially develop your own web. You can develop your own value and you can just attract people to come to you. If I am on Facebook and I am sending out posts with valued information, not trying to essentially recruit people, I am going to have that information passed around to my friends and to their friends. Social media has really changed everything for everybody, and the people who don't recognize this are being left behind.

You can build substantial lists and generate substantial leads through automating your social media marketing techniques and developing a very strategic linkage between all of your networks. By strategizing the information you are sending out, how you are sending it, when you are sending it, and why are you sending it; you can develop all the leads that you need to build your business. You don't have to get out there and start paying thousands of dollars to do direct-response marketing. It's not required. You can build a substantial list, you can build a substantial business, and you can offer substantial value through social media marketing. You can allow these tools to constantly brand you on an on-going basis.

If you are doing direct-response marketing, you are going to get a much larger influx of leads. If you are just doing the influx of leads, chances are you are going to get a whole bunch of volume and interest in that product in the beginning. Yet, you always want to en-

Jason O'Toole

sure that if you are bringing people in through direct-response marketing, you've got to back-end the social media funnel system that you put people through, so you can be developing those relationships. You want to develop the "know, like, and trust" model because on the Internet you've got to be exposing your opportunity or your product forty times. In traditional marketing, it will be seven times. But in relationship marketing it is only three times and this is why most companies have that three-step process – because this is the number for relationship marketing.

> "Learn the philosophy of always giving. Always be looking to help other people achieve their goals...and that in turn is what is going to make you an attractive marketer."

So, as long as you've got a system that can funnel people into a back-end system that constantly is branding you and getting your ads in front of their face thirty-nine more times to really make it worth your while, then direct-sales marketing is great. But you don't *need* it.

Q. **Is there anything else you want to share with an aspiring networker or attraction marketer?**

A. Focus on relationships and just being abundant. Focus on friendships and stop trying to sell. Offer value every time you send something out via your social networks or via your email list. Always put yourself in other people's shoes. Really ask yourself, "If I was on Joe's list, or if I was a friend of Joe's on Twitter and I was following him, or if I was a friend of his on Facebook, what value does this information provide me? Am I going to be excited about this information? Is it going to help me?" Don't constantly send out information directing people to a sales page.

Learn the philosophy of always giving. Always be looking to help other people achieve their goals, achieve what they are going to do, and that in turn is what is going to make you an attractive marketer. This is someone people will see as a friend for life; someone who is going to help them get through road blocks for their business. Someday down the road, if they are looking for a coach or a mentor, or things go wrong for them; who are they going to think of? Who are they going to look toward to hear about a new business if they are looking to switch businesses?

When you reach this level of an elite attraction marketer, that's when people are contacting you because you are a trusted resource to them. You may have never met them before. I get people that call me all the time – I don't know who these people are, but they know me and it's more than that. They know me, they like me, and they trust me because they read my information. They read the things I post, they value the videos we post, and they are seeing success with it; so they look at us as trusted resources in the industry as a whole.

It's these people that call me and take the initiative to get a hold of me; to get to know me. These are the people I reciprocate and start to develop friendships with. This is essentially attraction marketing.

Summary
- Stop trying to sell
- Stop working out of desperation because that's what you are doing when you are always chasing your family and friends. Stop chasing!
- Attractive networkers understand that others work with them because of the value they offer
- Every time you send something out via your

social networks or via your email list, always put yourself in other people's shoes

- Always give more than you ever expect in return
- Focus on friendships, relationships and just being abundant
- Simply talk to people with no ulterior motive or agenda whatsoever
- Take ownership of your business; pick and choose who you work with
- Don't give people the power to control how you feel about something
- Develop leadership in your team
- Online networking methods are, for me, a lead generation strategy
- Developing the long-term aspect of your organization absolutely requires an offline component
- Become the person you wish to recruit and stop trying to recruit the person you're trying to become

JASON O'TOOLE'S RECOMMENDED RESOURCES

- YourProxpex.com – Jason's system
- *Brilliant Compensation* – Tim Sales

JASON O'TOOLE'S RECOMMENDED RESOURCES ONLINE

http://50networkers.com/jason-otoole

YOURPROSPEX.COM

SEVEN

I don't care how you do it, but get in front of somebody new as often as you can.

James Klingensmith,
Official Alice 105.9 FM
Radio Morning Show
Hypnotist

James grew up in Casper, Wyoming (population of approximately 50,000 people) and lived there until he was about 23 years old. He had a full ride voice scholarship to a state college and then went to the Hypnosis Motivation Institute in Tarzana, California.

James has been in sales and networking for most of his life. From the age of seven on, James has been an award-winning salesman. He was the kid who always sold the most candy bars for fundraisers. Through the years, James has sold newspapers, choir and drama tickets. At age 14 he started selling lumber, cabinets and repairs for Builder's Mark. He did this for the next 10 years. James drove a Schwan's truck on a commission only basis and became the number one salesperson, doubling his route. From there, he went on to be a broker at a car business becoming employee of the month – the only salesperson to be awarded that distinction for this organization. He then went to work for Service Magic and was in the top 4 of 400 sales people, outselling pretty much everybody.

According to James, "Working in sales is all the same no

matter what the product or service is. You sell yourself, which is the most important part. If somebody will buy you, they will buy your product." This is where James' style fits in with networking and attraction marketing. He is marketing himself first, rather than his service, and people buy the service because they buy him as a person.

I met James in a leads group where he opened with a short presentation by standing on a chair and singing an aria. A novel approach for me, and definitely a memorable one. If I tried that for an introduction, it would be memorable for a different reason! James launched full-time into his hypnotherapy counseling practice in February 2009 after gradually building his client base through word-of-mouth, referrals and relationships, without paid advertising.

You can find out more about James Klingensmith at AskYourHypnotist.com.

Q. Have any of your prior jobs helped you develop skills beneficial to your networking activities?

A. From the day that you are born to the day that you die, you network. Even with your parents, and the friends they have, you network as you grow up. You find out how to respond to them, how to get what you want, and how to get what you need. You just

> *"Working in sales is all the same no matter what the product or service is. You sell yourself, which is the most important part. If somebody will buy you, they will buy your product."*

take these skills and expand on them; you don't hide in your box, and you treat everybody the way that you would want to be treated.

Q. **Was there a point where you sort of felt like you were more proficient in networking, or has it been an ongoing process of self-development?**

A. The cool thing about networking is that once you think you've got it figured out, you find out you have no clue about what is going on and you have to redo it all over again. Each and every person you meet is different.

Q. **What makes the difference between an attractive networker, a boring networker and an irritating networker?**

A. My favorite networker is the passionate person. The person who is completely passionate about what they do. You know you have found somebody who is completely passionate about something when they won't shut up about it. Anybody can be coached or trained to not say so much; to swallow their words a little bit more, but you can't train somebody to love what they do. That's the number one best. An irritating networker is somebody who doesn't care about their business; who just doesn't care about what they do or why they do it. If they don't love what they do, then maybe they should work by the hour. This irritates me. That's the two differences in life and networking.

Q. **What kind of things have you done consciously to improve your networking skills?**

A. I use hypnosis, which works subconsciously. I am consciously putting myself into a state of hypnosis and then subconsciously changing some things about me to become a better networker. Another one is leads groups. I love *"I Take The Lead"* and leads groups in general.

Q. **What were the hardest networking skills that you have developed that have had the most impact on**

JAMES KLINGENSMITH

your success?

A. Computers! They've got to be the hardest for me. I do not spell, write, or type well. For some people, they're easier; for me, they're horrifying.

Q. **Was there anything that was a turning point in your networking development? Something where the light came on and you went, "Wow, this is great. This is something that really works."**

A. Probably in high school when I sold more drama tickets than anybody else. The drama teacher – Mr. Sidelly; I still remember him and I still stay in contact with him, came up to me one night and personally thanked me for helping out the drama club. That's what it was all about. It was about developing this relationship and it was about making somebody, besides me, happy.

Q. **Do you suggest finding a good marketing coach, mentor or mastermind group?**

A. The reality is you get what you pay for. If you spend $300 to get somebody's advice, you are going to get $300 of somebody's advice. If you spend your time with somebody who actually knows how to do it, does it well, and you shadow that person, your time is more valuable than any money you could throw down on the ground. That's probably the best. Coaches and stuff? Sure, they have good ideas, but you get what you pay for. Experience is number one; trial and error is number two.

Go out and fail! Try rejection over and over again. Get slapped in the face a few times; get told "no." Get it so bad that you get to the point where rejection actually starts feeling good, and then – and only then – will you start to learn. I could tell you to do a million things right now, but until you actually start doing them, it doesn't make any difference, and you know that as well as me.

Q. Do you have any particular recommended training resources, books, classes, anything like that which come to mind?

A. Hypnosis, hypnosis, hypnosis! Use your mind. I said it right into the camera because you really need to use your mind; use your brain. All those other classes; like I said before, you get what you paid for. The main thing is: You want to find out how to use your mind and body to work for you. Once you can actually figure this out for the most part, how to open up your mind and make your mind control your body instead of your body controlling your mind, then you can actually take control of the reins of your life.

The cool thing about hypnotherapists is that they're not like regular therapists: You don't need them all your life. You only need them for a few months at most and then, that's pretty much it. So, hypnosis, hypnosis, hypnosis. Oh, and God! I should put God in there. Religion is big, whatever religion it is. I respect everyone's religion; everyone has a right to choose their religion and everything else. But I truly believe you have to believe in something bigger than yourself to become successful, because when you put all the weight of the world on your own shoulders, well, it's pretty hard to walk.

Q. Did you ever feel overwhelmed with all of the things you had to learn or improve on to achieve the success you desired? How did you work through that?

A. Well, sure. When I was in seventh grade, I was probably the most stressed person you would ever meet. I was so stressed that I had headaches every day. I was the guy who got shoved into lockers. I was the guy who got duct taped. It's not that nobody liked me. It's

James Klingensmith

just that I was really small and easy to take advantage of.

I learned then, how to take care of and control my stress. So sure, it gets overwhelming. But as long as I take a deep breath, relax, let the air all blow out, take the stress and throw it away, then I am fine. Most people take the stress inside. I was blessed to discover how to de-stress at an early age.

Q. Looking back now, is there anything you wish you had learned or done sooner?

A. Yes, I wish I would have known hypnosis going through grade school. Maybe I wouldn't have gotten shoved into all those lockers!

Q. If I had 30 minutes a day to devote to improving my networking and attractive marketing skills, what would you recommend I do with that time?

A. Self-hypnosis; 100%, self-hypnosis. Put yourself in a state of hypnosis and actually reorganize your mind and reorganize your day. Go through your day completely, as you are in that hypnosis state, and change your unknowns and your fears. Get rid of them. Throw them completely away. Also become more powerful; become more in touch with your own mind. Use your mind for what it is. If you only have 15 to 30 minutes – do hypnosis. Prayer counts as hypnosis for this exercise; you are still in the same state when you pray.

Q. A lot is said about having a catchy 30-second elevator speech that you can deliver confidently. What is your perspective on this?

A. Of course it's important! You bet! People believe in love at first sight. People believe in a first impression – it's 100% true, 1,000% true. The reason why it is so true is because this is how you are remembered. There are associations that you have in those first 15 to 30 seconds with a person, and that's what you are going to remember them by. It takes a lot to change that association.

Q. When you are in a networking situation in a mixture of leads groups or whatever, how important is it to be yourself?

A. I am glad you asked me that. It is extremely important not to fake it. A lot of people say, "Fake it until you make it." The truth of the matter is, don't fake it until you make it. Just actually believe that it is going to happen and you will find, more often than not, that it will.

Q. In a chance meeting, someone asks you what you do, what might you say that takes less than 30 seconds?

A. What do I do? I might say that "I make dreams come true." I am a hypnotherapist in Denver, Colorado. I aspire to be the number one hypnotherapist in Colorado. "Who do you know who wants to improve their life?" I can say it just like that. I will open up the reins and get the conversation started.

Q. Confidence and professionalism can be attractive traits; is there a danger that your practiced, 30-second elevator speech could come off as slick or glib?

A. We always have to keep working on that. No matter what I say, you have time to listen for 15 seconds. So it doesn't matter if it comes off slick or not, as long as you ask the question at the end on how it might benefit them, or how it is going to work for

> *"It is extremely important not to fake it...Just actually believe that it is going to happen and you will find, more often than not, that it will."*

them. You know the real goal of the elevator speech, of the 15-second speech, is to benefit the other person. It has nothing to do for you. If someone asks a question; they deserve an honest answer.

Q. **You seem to have a lot of different styles of your own business cards; I think that's version number three that I have seen.**

A. Yes, I have quite a few business cards. This is for one reason only. When people put my cards in their book or index, I want them to go ahead and put my cards in different spots so other people have a chance to see them. For example, if I let you look through my business card book here, you would be able to see my friends and also my card there. I do quite a few different things, especially with hypnosis. This one here says, "Fix your money problems." It's a conversational starter. This one says, "Stop Smoking." Another one is just general. I have one that says, "Self Improvement." There are a lot of different things we do, but when I am talking to somebody I find that it is important to talk about just one thing at a time. That way I don't get everything out there all at once. So you can have different cards that specialize with one thing each.

Q. **What is more important, your skills, your personality, posture, being able to provide value to people, being a good listener or having a catchy 30-second elevator speech?**

A. Passion, passion, passion. And more passion! All the rest doesn't really matter. As long as that person believes in what they do so much that they almost take it to the next level, or actually take it to the next level. This is evangelism for what they do. You will find that the best networkers out there don't need to have the best language, stories or testimonials. They just need to love what they do with a deep passion.

Q. Sometimes it can seem overwhelming with so many new things to learn and think about. Are people generally fairly forgiving as a new networker stumbles through the learning process?

A. Oh yes, yes, yes, yes. People are more forgiving than you would ever think of. In fact, you are your own worst critic.

Q. Are there any particular mistakes people make that are unforgivable in networking?

A. Yes! There are quite a few of them actually. One is offensive jokes. Be careful if your jokes are too offensive. This is very important. Remember that first 15 seconds? It is the first 15 seconds you meet somebody that makes their first impression; that's how they see you. It's very important. Make sure that you know who you are talking to as well. In fact, it's okay to be shy; it's okay to be quiet. Here's the best thing for somebody brand new: keep your mouth shut and your ears open. Listen and learn.

Q. Online networking, offline networking: is one better than the other or is it a matter of personal style and skills?

A. They are both very, very important – I am online with everything from my phone to my laptop. So what is more important? There is a ton of value online, but I say going outside is more important. When you actually have that physical connection with another human being, there's almost some type of chemistry about it that you can't get online. It doesn't matter if it's just one-on-one, a small group, or a large group, as long as I am outside the house and my hands meet somebody else's hands or my eyes are in contact with somebody else's eyes; that's where I want to be.

Q. Do you find social media to be a distraction or a ben-

James Klingensmith

OFFICIAL ALICE 105.9 FM RADIO MORNING SHOW HYPNOTIST

efit for your business?

A. 100% benefit, because I can update things all the time. It's all about being found and people can find me a lot easier.

Q. **If I was just starting out with my brand new company or as a new associate or employee for an established company, what is the best use of time initially to start developing my networking skills?**

A. Getting out of the house! You can't sell to anybody who is just in your store unless you are a retail store. Most of us aren't retail. I don't care where you go, just get outside and talk to somebody.

Q. **If you had a slogan to live by or something you would put on your tombstone, what would it be?**

A. Well, hopefully, if it was written on my tombstone, "Jesus lives." It really goes back to my Christian roots there. I want to be an example to other Christians; this is important to me. So something along that line, or "He was a good Christian."

Q. **Do you have written goals or a personal mission statement?**

A. Being a Christian is number one in my life, and goals are second. My written goals are probably different than most. My number one written goal is to be the best hypnotherapist in Colorado; it's written out, it's played out pretty much everywhere I go. I see a reminder of it every single day. A mission statement? Really, the Bible took care of that for me – John 3:16. This is about the best mission statement you can do.

Q. **How important is it to be clear about your personal and business core values in relating to people in a networking context?**

A. Integrity is number one. If you say you are going to

be somewhere, be there. You do that at the minimum. If you do what you say you are going to do, you're always going to be the hero.

Q. How do you attract quality people into your network who might be good power partners, peer advisors or joint venture partner? People you can trust your referrals to, or people who might refer others to you.

A. I am going to put another spin on this – do you mind? Here's what I love: I love it when somebody makes a mistake. I love it when somebody accidentally does something to make somebody else, especially me – upset, because this is what tells me how they are going to fix the problem.

How they are going to fix the problem is very important to me. It gives me an idea of how they are going to fix a problem with someone else I refer to them. Everybody is going to have problems; we know this. How do they take care of a problem? Do they shove it under the rug, do they shout at you, or do they fix it? That's where I find my power partners right there.

> *"It doesn't matter what somebody does – I could care less if the guy shovels snow or if the guy is an acupuncturist. The only thing that matters is how they fix problems."*

It doesn't matter what somebody does – I could care less if the guy shovels snow or if the guy is an acupuncturist. The only thing that matters is how they fix problems.

Q. So you are basically saying that anyone can do a good job when things go well, but when things don't go as planned, that's what separates a quality partner from

James Klingensmith

somebody who is maybe not so good.

A. Exactly! Of course, a power partner is going to be somebody who does pretty much what you do. Or what you do and what they do go hand-in-hand. That's a partner. But again, you've got to take both sides of the coin on that too, so get them to mess up! I am just kidding; don't get them to mess up. It's going to happen.

Q. **Does letting go of any emotional expectation of a sale, or personal agenda from a networking interaction, free you to have a more successful interaction?**

A. No! Assume the sale. I know people say don't assume, but the reality is, you should always assume the sale! Don't get emotionally attached to the sale. Instead, get physically attached to it. Believe that you have that sale and whether you have it or not, it doesn't matter. You have to believe that you are going to have that sale, emotionally and physically, before somebody is going to give you their money. Does that make more questions?

Q. **It does, but that's good. That's why I am here. Well, let's say that you are a hypnotherapist and your specialty is helping people stop smoking. When you are talking to someone and maybe they smoke, maybe they don't; you don't know at this point. If you get all caught up about having this person become your client to stop them smoking, can that put them on the defensive, where they may not think of referring other people to you, because you are in their face too much?**

A. I see what you are saying. You are saying, "Do I jump the gun?" No, absolutely not. I am always closing. I always ask for their business and I always close. The way I do that is to remember that it's not about the money. It's never been about money. None of this networking stuff is about money. If you have integrity and do what you say you are going to do, you are going to make all the money you need.

The reality is that becoming your client is not what you are closing someone on. For example, let's take a smoker, like you said. If that smoker comes to me and they are not ready to quit smoking, I really don't want that person in my chair. The reason why I don't want that person is because I don't want to take their money at all. But I want to talk to them and I want to close them on the idea of recommending somebody that they know. I always want to keep closing them and closing them, but not on the money part. In fact, the money part is so minute when it comes to sales. So minute! Does this make sense?

Q. So you are using a much broader definition of a sale to be not just a monetary transaction, it's winning a relationship with someone or it's winning a positive direction?

A. No. It's not about winning either; it's just closing. Do you see what I mean?

Q. Not really. What do you mean?

A. When it comes to closing, what you want to do is to be in agreement with the other person. When you are in agreement with the other person, you can get comfortable with them. It is all about getting comfortable with that other person. That's why NLP (Neuro-Linguistic Programming) and the study of unconscious traits exist. When you are comfortable with that other person, you've closed the deal. That person is comfortable with you and you are comfortable with them. When you are comfortable with someone, you trust that person. Comfort is number one. Am I making more sense now? **Yes.**

JAMES KLINGENSMITH

Okay. You see how you answered yes there? That's the other thing I like to do; I like to ask people questions like that over and over again and just find out where we are. Are we on the same track or not? That's closing, believe it or not. It's closing, closing, closing, closing, and when you close, all you do is you close the door to that subject and go onto the next because you are both in agreement. Once you both are in agreement, you keep going up and up, and then at the final state, after you've done what you said you are going to do; you take the money. There's always money for the taking, always.

Q. How do you handle fear of rejection?

A. I love getting rejected. In the way you think about rejection, I love it, and I will tell you why: it empowers me so much. Number one, it gives me a challenge. Number two, half the time; rejection is not a "no". In fact, if you look, almost 80% of the time, you are not hearing a "no," you are just hearing an objection.

This is where you go to work, where you get to have fun, and go to the next level. You find a common interest, a comfortable spot that you have with that person, and keep moving them up and up. I love rejection – love it!

Q. And this works the same with friends or strangers? You don't take things more personally with friends?

A. Well, of course I do. I am human, just like anybody else. The more of a friend you are, the less I am going to see you as a client. Because, just like in my early life, the only thing I can help a kid with using hypnosis, are sports, theatre, and stuff like that. I don't do any of the therapy or anything like that with friends and their families because, the closer a friend you are, the less I am really going to talk to you about business.

Q. Do you get a lot of your customers through referrals or do you get some through advertising?

A. I do no advertising; only word of mouth. Networking, referrals, leads groups, talking to other people, knowing people they know and just talking, talking, talking. Lots of phone calls, relationships, and that's pretty much it.

For a therapist of any kind, it's going to be primarily networking and referrals. It's not about advertising; it's not about getting your name in the newspaper. But at the same time, I don't mind dropping a business card in an ashtray every time I walk by one.

Q. Do you think that luck and timing have anything to do with success in networking and attraction marketing? Or are there one or two other factors that play a big part for you?

A. That's the best question I have heard yet! Luck and timing... People always blame it on luck and timing. Sure, why not, let's say yes and break this down... Here's what really happens: every single second your eyes and your body get over a billion messages that go to your brain. It's just amazing. Now, not all of them can compute or fit in there, so your brain has to decide what it is going to throw away and what to keep up there. So you can actually re-program your brain – which is amazing, and find the thing they call 'luck', and take in all the opportunities that you missed before.

Let's get a good example... Sometimes in a leads group somebody will be saying, "Oh man, I need to lose weight," or "My wife needs to lose weight," or, "My cholesterol is over the top," or something like that. You might not even hear that because you haven't programmed your mind to listen and catch it. Believe it or not, you can miss it all the time. So, it's all about what your mind chooses to accept. You create your own luck from that. You create your own timing. It's amazing – there is money out there every single day. There is so much money for people to have and it just comes to you if your train your mind to look for it.

Q. So luck is really a heightened perception of opportunities that are already there?

A. Man, he says it better than I, doesn't he? I love it!

Q. What have been the biggest rewards for you from your networking activities?

A. When I help change somebody's life. It doesn't matter if they are a client, or whatever happened. If their life is better because they met me, this is the biggest reward. I can give you example after example after example, but when those things happen, there's nothing better.

Q. What have been your biggest challenges?

A. Challenges? My 18 month old son is my biggest challenge, because while I am out here doing this, I am not making any money. Truthfully, I have told you that money will come if you do everything that's right. Obviously I don't have an appointment today, but I do tomorrow and the next day. During these networking things, I have to take him over to the babysitter and that's hard for anybody.

Q. How do you keep your team motivated?

A. Inspiration and testimonials. The more you can tell about yourself – that's how you get people motivated.

Q. How important is follow-up to a professional networker or attraction marketer?

A. That's all a professional networker does; follow-up.

Somebody who is a professional networker always follows up – they call back, and they call back. It's huge; it's everything! This is networking.

Q. What are the most effective ways you have found to follow up with people?

A. Telephone, coffee, their idea, or meeting like we are here. Anything that they give you as an excuse to get in front of them; you definitely want to find that opportunity! If it's a person who doesn't have any passion about their business, find somebody who does. The more people you get in front of, the better. Just call, email, and touch base with them. Here's another one: after that first month and you've established that first impression well, then you can follow up with them anytime. You can call them up after six months, "Do you remember me?" But you've got to get that first impression in there tight and get in front of them again, in my opinion.

Q. What is your attitude towards competition?

A. I love competition. Having somebody advertise for you for free – how nice is that? "Bring it on!"

For the most part, if there is competition, there is more than one person besides just you shouting out about your product or service and getting somebody's attention. The more people we can get into hypnosis, the better. There's plenty of money for everybody out there. Don't stop, bring it on. I want competition.

Q. How do you maintain a perspective that serves you in these tough times? No doubt, you occasionally hear about other business owners sharing their struggles with the economy. Do you allow yourself to get pulled into that downward spiral? How do you keep your head up?

A. There's enough money to go around. They are printing just as much money today as they printed yesterday, honestly. That's the reality. There's as much gold in the world, actually, there is more gold in the world today, more diamonds in the world today, more money in the world today than there was yesterday, a year ago, or even ten years ago. They always keep finding money; I am not worried about it at all. I believe that if you have the attitude where you get what you give, and there's enough to go around, then you will be fine.

Q. **Is there anything else you want to share with an aspiring networker or attraction marketer?**

A. Yeah, we have two ears and only one mouth. Listen, listen, listen, and pay attention. Knock on doors, get out of the house, get out of the office, go meet somebody new, and go shake everybody's hand. Give a stranger a smile, make eye contact – I don't care how you do it, but get in front of somebody new as often as you can.

SUMMARY

- I could tell you to do a million things, but until you actually start doing them, it doesn't make any difference
- You sell yourself. If somebody will buy you, they will buy your product
- Get in front of somebody new as often as you can
- The associations that you make, in the first 15-30 seconds that you have with a person, is what they will remember you by
- It takes a lot to change the first associations but you've got to establish that first impression well, and get in front of them again
- Somebody who is a professional networker al-

ways follows up
- The real goal of the elevator speech is to benefit the other person. They ask a question; they deserve an honest answer
- Networking is about developing relationships and making somebody happy besides you
- I am consciously putting myself into a state of hypnosis and then subconsciously changing some things about me to become a better networker
- Open up your mind and make your mind control your body instead of your body controlling your mind
- My favorite networker is the person who is completely passionate about what they do
- For somebody brand new: keep your mouth shut and your ears open. Listen and learn
- Integrity is number one. Do what you say you are going to do
- It is important to talk about one thing at a time. Don't get everything out there all at once
- When you close, all you do is you close the door to that subject and go onto the next because you are both in agreement
- Luck is really a heightened perception of opportunities that are already there
- I love competition. Having somebody advertise for you for free – how nice is that?
- Have the attitude that you get what you give, and there is enough to go around

James Klingensmith's recommended resources online

http://50networkers.com/james-klingensmith

James Klingensmith

EIGHT

A ttractive networkers provide people with great value, whether they choose to be in business with them, or not.
Ty Tribble, Blogger and Social Media Entrepreneur

At the time of this writing, one of Ty Tribble's blogs (www. mlmblog.net) holds the number one spot on Google for both the search terms "MLM blog" and "network marketing blog". This is quite an accomplishment, given the number of sites and blogs on those topics.

Ty grew up in Seattle, Washington and has lived on the western side of Washington state for pretty much his whole life. Ty was raised alone for the most part by what he smilingly calls his somewhat "hippie" single mother until the age of seven, when his little brother came along. Ty was predisposed to be independent and caught the entrepreneurial spirit at a young age. Ty currently celebrates his freedom in being able to choose where he spends his time based on his own personal preferences and family needs, rather than being required to live in a specific locale for his work or business.

He attended Washington State University on the east side of the state to become a teacher. Ty did not actually finish college, although he is a big believer in college and education – both of his children will be going to college. At some

135

point, Ty had the revelation that he was not going to be able to meet the financial goals that he had set out for his family if he continued down the teaching route. He was already earning part-time what he would earn as a teacher, even after five years of teaching.

Ty has thought about going back to college at some point, but according to him, college is not useful from an Internet marketing perspective. Even if they put a curriculum together today, it would be very different in six weeks. College prepares you to go out and get a job, which is great for people who do great work and really enjoy what they do. Ty chose a different path. He wanted to make enough money in what he does for a living so that he could do what he wants in life.

> *"The great thing about being an entrepreneur is that I can really live anywhere I want to in the world and have frankly chosen to stay in Washington."*

After his brief time at college, Ty spent some time in corporate America, and had a very successful career before going full-time into his entrepreneurial ventures. Somewhere in the back of his mind, there was always the desire to work for himself, call his own shots, and not have a ceiling there to hit. He wanted to be able to triple his income in a year if he chose, rather than settle for a 5% raise.

His first job out of college was in the clothing business as a part-time worker who quickly moved up the ranks to help manage the facility. He moved to another garment manufacturing company and built up his reputation as a manager. Soon after, he became involved in the network marketing industry for the first time. He was able to put a lot of the skills he learned in network marketing to good use in the corporate managerial world. Ty worked for three

Blogger and Social Media Entrepreneur

different startup companies and was able to propel himself through the ranks because of personal development (people skills and leadership skills), that he developed in network marketing. He was easily reading approximately a book a week at the time, putting the tried and true principles he was learning into action in his daily work. This was helpful in setting him apart – even from people with higher levels of education.

Ty remarks that there seems to be a principle lost in the younger generations, and even his own generation. "Some people have this idea that they should achieve a certain level of success just by showing up. I always had the idea that I am going to work as hard and do as good a job as possible so that people will see that I am going above and beyond. I suspected that my income would begin to rise to match the level of excitement and enthusiasm I put toward it, as well as the sheer amount of work that I put toward it, and it certainly did."

> *"...my income would begin to rise to match the level of excitement and enthusiasm I put toward it, as well as the sheer amount of work that I put toward it, and it certainly did."*

Although Ty's network marketing experiences helped him make great strides in the corporate world, he initially struggled to make network marketing itself work for him. For five years he worked with the wrong company and the wrong mentorship before taking a five year break from that industry all together. Eighteen months after he returned to the network marketing industry, he hit his first home run and has been at a very high income level within the industry as a whole since that point. It has been for Ty, a wild ride for sure, but by no means an overnight success.

Q. How long were you involved in networking or attraction marketing before you actually started to see some tangible results for your business?

A. When I came back to the network marketing industry, it was 18 months before I hit a six figure income. This was with the proper mentorship and really taking what I did best and applying it to my business. This is a big tip. I did it in a pretty short period of time because I think I was mature enough. I also had a tremendous mentor in my life and a coach who was not afraid to call me and have uncomfortable conversations with me once in a while. They were uncomfortable for me at least; I am sure they were uncomfortable with him too, but they were really guiding conversations. In other words, "You are going in this direction. I highly recommend you make a change and reverse your course a little bit to get back on track." These conversations, again, were paramount to getting me to a successful level in a short period of time.

Q. Were there any significant milestones or turning points along the way?

A. Yes, without a question. It was just this lightning bolt experience of being in the shower, I tend to do a lot of thinking in the shower, and thinking to myself, "People don't simplify things enough." I remember thinking about one of my first forays into online marketing which was with Google AdWords in 2003. It was a drastically different place to be then, than it is today. It was the very beginning of Google AdWords.

My current business partner, Bo Short, was affiliated with a particular company and resigned at a very high level. I had found him and I had found him online. So I felt like there has got to be people that are searching for the same kind of things that I searched for when I found Bo.

I had a couple of very specific search terms and thought, "Okay, if I can make one of my ads come up at the top with a pay-per-click (PPC) campaign, I have the potential to create some great leads." I knew nothing about a lead capture page, a squeeze page, or anything related to capturing leads. I literally sent people directly to my goofy network marketing company replicated website.

I actually had the company make a couple of changes so it made a little more sense. I had them put our phone number and my email address on it so people could at least contact us; there was really no other way to do it. I began to enroll some big numbers. If you think about it, I was doing Google AdWords under the name of probably the second largest network marketing company in the world, and one of the largest in the U.S. at the time, for sure, and I was paying $0.05 per click. So I didn't really have to be very good at it because I was paying next to nothing for those PPC leads. So just being an early adopter in that arena got my feet wet a bit.

I will back up just a little bit. My wife and I, prior to that time, had the second largest eBay business in the state of Washington. We sold women's clothing over the Internet through our own website and through eBay. I had learned a little bit about Internet marketing as a result of this; I also learned a little bit about copywriting. I would write the ads for the clothing that went online. I would do a lot of things of this nature, so I began to think about the opportunity to apply what I had learned to this business of network marketing.

Interestingly, the previous company I was affiliated was like, "Wow, wow, wow; no, no, no – you have to do it the old-school way. There's no other way to do it, otherwise it doesn't duplicate," which is really a crock of you know what. It's the biggest lie in network marketing – that the things you can do on the Internet don't duplicate to your team. In fact they are very duplicate-able to your team.

I was kind of being held back in the other company because, even though they would claim that they are an Internet company, we weren't allowed to do anything on the Internet. Looking back, this was kind of funny! Then I met Bo Short. He became my mentor and I was actually affiliated with his company. When it came to other ways to build, he was very empowering. So I was kind of on the cutting edge of Google AdWords and that was really my first foray into the technology side. Later on I launched a blog and that's probably another story in itself.

Q. **What makes the difference between an attractive networker, a boring networker and an irritating networker?**

A. That's a great question; I love that. I think attractive networkers provide people with great value whether they choose to be in business with them or not. They are looked upon as a resource.

Boring networkers aren't providing value or making an offer whatsoever, so they are not telling you to get into their deal.

It's interesting to me: I've got an annoying networker that just drives me batty. He absolutely provides no value to anyone. Every single pitch he makes is, "Get in now, retire, sign up today. Get rich." And I am like, "Really? Do people really fall for that? This is your whole, entire pitch?" And I get an email, almost once a week, pitching his deal. He provides no value whatsoever to people who don't decide to get into his deal, and then who knows what he is providing in terms of value to people who are already in his deal. His whole attitude – "Get in and retire" – I mean…it's just annoying as hell.

Deal-jumpers drive me batty too. The same guy I bet has been in no less than 12 deals in the last month, but the next one is always "the one." So these guys bother me. There are very specific reasons to leave a company. Three times I have left companies and they were for very specific reasons. Was I sad that I had to move? Yes. Was it a very difficult decision? Absolutely! Will people look at me differently because I have moved between companies and been with four companies in the last 18 years? Probably! But were they the right decisions to make? Yes. There are specific reasons why you would want to leave a company. Overall, if you want to build a long-term income, go home from the dance with the date that brought you, unless that date is absolutely the wrong company.

> *"…you want to truly be someone who is very attractive to other people, and be able to provide great value."*

Ty Tribble

These are the basics: you want to truly be someone who is very attractive to other people, and be able to provide great value. I also don't think it hurts to be entertaining. When I talk about social media, I give people a couple of tips. Don't be boring. Then, don't talk about your business 24-7. These are the two biggest tips I give to people when it comes directly to social media because people don't care! Even if you have the most interesting job in the world and we are at a cocktail party, if you corner me in the kitchen and rapid fire on me about your job, it will be boring after a while. Well why in the world do people think this will work in social media when talking about their network marketing company? I don't want to hear about their network marketing company 24 hours a day, 7 days a week. But, when their 9-year-old does something cool; I'd love to hear about that!

Social media is very voyeuristic in nature. It's like reality TV and everybody can be their own star if they choose to do so. So overall, just be yourself, but be the most interesting version of yourself that you've got at this point! Then, provide great value and you are going to certainly attract people.

Q. **What kind of things have you done consciously to improve your networking skills?**

A. Oh, this is an easy one: read. I am a big student. I literally, over the last six months, got rid of hundreds of books because I bought one of these Amazon Kindles. I am the kind of guy that might read three books at once and my Kindle allows me to take them everywhere in a really compact package. Reading has been invaluable.

Listening to audio programs. Anything I can get my hands on related to Internet marketing and network marketing, I spend a lot of money on products in terms of training materials every year. I probably spend more money on training materials then the average network marketer makes in a year, and probably some of what the better network marketers make in a year. I feel like if I continually work on myself through personal development and continuous learning, I will not only be a better person, but will also be able to empower more people to go on to success. So, personal development and self-development are vital and I do them consciously on a regular basis. If I am not read-

BLOGGER AND SOCIAL MEDIA ENTREPRENEUR

ing one or two books a week, I am behind the curve.

And here's another thing that a lot of people miss. I think people are a little bit scared to opt into a free newsletter. There are a lot of different newsletters you can opt into online. If you are on a bunch of them, it will keep your mail box busy; but what if you can get just one idea from them for free?

I am absolutely baffled that someone would go through four or five of my MLM (Multi-Level Marketing) secrets emails and then opt out. It actually makes no sense whatsoever, because I know for a fact that the content in those MLM web secrets is so powerful that if someone takes all seven and applies them to their business, they are going to drive way more traffic to their site. Then they will make more money, and sponsor more people. It's a proven fact. So why someone would opt out when there is absolutely nothing being sold in those emails right now, absolutely blows me away.

I get the sense that people are afraid to request free information. I request all the free information I can get. If the up sell or whatever the person is selling makes sense, I will probably buy it too. Here's something very interesting; this is a big deal! Todd Falcone, a friend of mine who is a seven-figure income earner, had this to say on the topic; "If you are not open to someone selling you something of great value that will help you become a better person, or become better in your chosen field, such as training materials or something like that; how in the world could you possibly expect your potential business partners or prospects to be open to what you have to offer them?"

Interesting, isn't it? So if you don't have this openness

Ty Tribble

to buying, why in the world would someone be open to buy from you? It's not super-deep, but at the same time I think it makes a lot of sense.

I subscribe to every free piece of material that I can possibly get and many times I will buy additional material. I've got a library of downloaded material that has gig, after gig of information – I had to buy a couple of separate mega-gigabyte hard drives to hold all the stuff that I have purchased. If I can just get one or two ideas out of those things, and teach them to other people, it is well worth the money.

So you ask, "How did you learn all this stuff?" Well, I learned it through massive study. I developed my own style and process by pulling an idea from here and an idea from there. All of a sudden I have something that is maybe different from what other people are doing, but is a cumulative result of a lot of different ideas, and a lot of different training and teaching.

I am a big believer in what Mr. Swanson, one of my high school math teachers, once said: "Good teachers borrow ideas, but great teachers steal them." I always try to give credit to wherever the ideas come from. But a lot of what I do is a result of pulling ideas from many different sources; and some of them are free. It pains me to see people so un-open to gathering information about this industry when one of those little ideas could make a drastic change in their business overall.

Q. **Do you have any particular recommended training resources, books, classes, anything like that which come to mind?**

A. The first thing I would do is buy a book called *Crush It*. That book will kind of give you a good overview about social media.

I think if you want some basics in terms of attraction marketing, I would get Mike Dillard's *Magnetic Sponsoring* and Ann Sieg's Renegade Marketing. The interesting thing about these two products is that, although they are very similar in scope overall, one of them is actually going to relate to a younger, more male crowd, and the other one will relate to an older, more female crowd. If you want to have both those types of people in your business, it might not hurt to read both of them.

This would be a good place to start. One of the biggest problems today is that people don't know where to start online. They know they need to get online somehow but they don't know where to start. That is also one of the things I am working diligently on helping people with, right now.

If you want to get more in depth, I think Mike Dillard's *MLM Traffic Formula II* is excellent, as well as The *The Renegade Professional* – the monthly membership site with Ann Sieg and Mike Klingler, where you can go in and look at all the mass of vaulted training. I am not in *The Renegade Professional* once a day because I have a good idea of what I am doing. Even if I am in there only once a week or once a month, I pay about $50 a month – just like everyone else does, but if I can get one little tutorial that I can grab hold of and teach to my team, as well as apply to myself, it is worth it. This is such a fast-changing business that you've got to stay on top of what's going on. If not, you are going to be lost – I'm not saying you, but in general.

So I think those are two big ones, The *The Renegade Professional* and The *MLM Traffic Formula II*. They will cost money, but nothing from Mike Dillard or Ann Sieg, that I have ever purchased, has not been worth it.

Everything has been well worth it's time.

Then you know what? If you are smart, you will write a review of one on a blog and drive some traffic to the review from Facebook and Twitter. All of a sudden you can make enough affiliate commissions to pay for your product.

Q. Are there any particular mistakes people make that are unforgivable in networking?

A. Yeah, that's an interesting question, without a doubt. Here's the biggest thing: It's not that you are not going to put your family and your financial future ahead of other people. What drives me batty, is people who call themselves leaders and yet 99% of their followers are losing money every month; they are spending more money than they are making. This, to me, is not leadership. It is influence over people; however, it is not influence in the right way.

Then on top of that, they have some system that they are selling. When the system is outdated and not working, they claim people are not working hard enough and it is not the system's fault. They say the failure is that person's fault, which leads to tons, probably millions of people associated with the network marketing industry feeling like; "I am a loser and I never made it." In reality it's not their fault, it is that they are being taught some of the wrong things and they are not being led by a leader who has their best interest at heart.

I struggled for 10 years in the network marketing industry in that kind of environment. Eighteen months after I got a true mentor, I was earning six figures. It wasn't me that changed dramatically. My mentorship changed, and I was affiliated with a different company. I think the biggest thing, and what drives me nuts, are people who don't have their team's best interest at heart.

Q. Online networking, offline networking: is one better than the other, do you need both, or is it a matter of personal style and skills?

A. A lot of people get involved in attraction marketing and networking and it's really quite interesting. People who have absolutely no clue about the Internet come up to me and say; "I want to build my business 100% online." Even I don't build my business 100% online. The fact of the matter is I have never met a single person in the history of networking marketing who has built a large, high-level income – high-level residual income – that does not build relationships with people. So there needs to be a very specific balance online and offline.

Q. So from your perspective, the online stuff is great for meeting people and just extending the sphere of people who recognize your name and have some contacts with you. But the real business is built through the real relationships that you have built since the initial contact?

A. It's not that you can't build relationships online; but at some point you have to extend beyond that if you want to build a long-term business. If you want to sell people a $3,000 package and never speak to them again, maybe you can do that without building relationships. But for me, I am building a long-term residual income with people who trust me; so that I could walk away from my business for six months and my income would go up. There is a different type of mentality when it comes to that. Here's the great thing about the Internet: you can reach more people faster than ever before in the history of our world. The problem with it is that people get this notion that the

Ty Tribble

Internet is an easier, better way. Frankly, this notion is perpetrated by a lot of really good marketing. It is certainly possible to do through online methods, but in the long run, you cannot discount the value of a relationship.

Bo Short, my business partner, is one of the very best I have ever met in my life, at cold contacting people. He created a CD that sold over a million copies in a company. On his very best day, he can't come anywhere near the sheer numbers in terms of the number of leads that I can generate on the Internet. But again, I think it should be a balance.

As a matter of fact I did it this morning. I had someone reach out to me via the Internet to talk about attraction marketing. They called me – which is one of the most wonderful feelings you will ever get in the history of your business when that happens for the first time. They called me and happened to be local enough that my wife and I got in our car and met them at their home. We all sat down and talked about business.

This is somewhat off-track but very much related. I believe God made us, people, in such a way that we like to interact with others; as opposed to sitting at home with our laptop on our bare legs, in our underwear, trying to build our businesses. I think we crave interaction with human beings, and I think it is a good thing. I am not trying to minimize my interaction with human beings; I am trying to maximize my productivity and make all of my interaction productive, but I like the human factor of what I do for a living.

Q. How do you attract quality people into your network who might be good power partners, peer advisors or joint venture partners? People you can trust your re-

ferrals to, or people who might refer others to you?

A. That's a good question. I think first of all you look for people who have similar values to you. I think that like-minded people will tend to congregate together a little bit in this industry, particularly online. Where does it start? It probably starts with your blog. How do people know what you believe if you are not writing about it on your blog? I think this will certainly help attract like-minded people to you overall. Then don't be afraid to pick up the phone.

If I find value from someone online, I will see if I can find their number, pick up the phone, call them, and say "Hi!" Art Jonak, for example, is a guy who has been around the industry for a long time. I think he has people's best interest at heart. I don't think he's got a big agenda; I think he loves to see people succeed. We spent an hour on the phone not long ago and not one time did I try to get him into anything I was doing and not one time did he try to get me into anything he was doing, but it was more about, "How can we help each other be better at our business, to become better leaders, to do things differently."

Here's the great thing about Facebook; if you are a friend of somebody on Facebook, you can go to their "info" and I believe, in many cases, you can find their phone number and do that.

If I have truly found value in what they do – I sometimes like to ask people, "Would a testimonial from me help you in any way, shape, or form?" I will offer to give someone a testimonial. Now believe me: I don't do this for everyone. I do it for people from whom I have found great value in what they are doing, especially on the Internet. Overall, it's a great gesture. I think of this as holding out an olive branch to people;

TY TRIBBLE

you never know what can come out of it.

So, if you continue to build your reputation and work to be the best you can be, then, when you need to call in some favors, it's easy. I have been alluding to a product that we have coming out. I have called a couple of people, and sent a handful of emails to people I have worked with in the past on various projects; maybe I posted an article for them or whatever the case may be. I say, "Hey, I am coming out with this. Do you think your list, your readers, people who are interested in what you are doing; would be interested in it?" In most cases the answer is, "Absolutely, we would love to promote something you came out with," because they know it is going to be solid.

Overall, it's about being yourself, being authentic, telling the truth. I think it is also about finding people who are like-minded in terms of ethics, integrity level, and where we all want to see this industry go.

Here is something that drives me nuts as well: you have a certain number of people who say, "We should never talk bad about other people or other companies in this industry because it brings the whole industry down."

I see so much hype and garbage. If people who are throwing this junk out there are not held accountable by their peers; who in the world is going to hold them accountable? So I have never been afraid to. A lot of you say, "Oh, you can't say stuff like that," or, "if someone does something wrong, you can't call them out." Here's the thing, for example: If a newspaper reports on someone who has robbed a bank; does the newspaper reporting on it harm the reputation of that person's family? Or did the person robbing the bank harm the reputation of that person's family? Well, it's the person who robbed the bank!

Collectively; let's do this the right way! We don't need companies out there handing people a bottle of their stuff and saying, "Here, try this. It will help you with your…" and then you insert a disease, such as arthritis or whatever. I mean, that's like an illegal claim and has all kinds of hype associated with it. I am an anti-hype guy and I wish people would just focus on doing the right thing and overall, as an industry, everybody will rise to the top without the hype.

The Internet has been a great thing for network marketers. It has also been a bad thing for network marketers; because no longer can someone sit across from somebody else at a coffee shop, and tell them all kinds of stuff that is not true. In the past, people have had nowhere to refute that information. Today they can go online and refute it immediately through the Internet. So it's a good thing and a bad thing. It's a good thing for the people that want to do this business right; I think it's a bad thing for the hype artists.

Q. Does letting go of any emotional expectation of a sale, or personal agenda from a networking interaction, free you to have a more successful interaction?

A. Without a doubt, but I will take that one step further. My product line is a nutritional-based product, so there are three product related areas that I focus on. Then there's income opportunity. What I teach people on my team is, rather than running around trying to pitch their deal to people, I teach them to be solution providers; to go out and solve problems. I would kid someone, and hand them a Q-tip to clean out their ears. The number one thing people need to do in network marketing is to listen to what is going on around them. Inevitably, people will identify themselves as potential business partners or potential customers to you, especially if you are in the right type of company.

In conversations you have with people, eventually they often identify themselves as needing some additional help. Perhaps from a financial perspective, or a health related perspective with my particular company. Maybe they want to lose weight, maybe they need overall health from an immune system perspective, or maybe it's an energy perspective. Maybe they are addicted to Red Bull or something like that – I have a solution for all four of those areas. So if I am chatting to someone and they say "Hey Ty, I set a New Year's resolution to lose 25 pounds and so far, since Jan 1st, I have gained five. Not so hot!" Now, if I offer that person a way to lose weight that has been proven – that we are seeing great results across the country with, and they say, "I wouldn't be interested in that," then there's no emotional attachment to it. It's their problem.

I offered them a solution. Now if they are not willing to accept my solution, it's not about me. It's not about getting into business with me, or buying from me, it's about them. Here's the problem: if you are focusing on what you experience in a conversation, how a person reacts to you in that conversation, or on if they are telling you "no", then you are focusing your eyes inwardly and you are not focusing on that other person.

To me, that is the biggest thing. If people can get over that hurdle and not run around and try to pitch all their friends on their deal, but rather solve problems – that's all a salesperson really does, the good ones at least.

I have a new Porsche 911 – great car, it's a convertible and I actually have the top down today. If you have the top down in March in the Seattle area, you know there is crazy weather going on. It is just a beautiful day and my wife and I were cruising down the freeway with the top down.

When I bought the car last October, I knew I wanted black, I knew I wanted a convertible, and I knew I wanted specific options. When I went to the car dealer and said, "Here's what I want." If he tried to say, "Well, I know that's what you want, but let me tell you something: I've got this Jaguar over there that is forest green and is a beautiful car. What's it going to take to get you into that today?" I would be like, "Dude, although I like Jaguars and I like the color green – this is the color that I want. This is the car that I need." Do you think I would be impressed with him then saying "Well, how about that orange Pinto?" or whatever?

This used-car mentality of "What is going to get you in the car today; what's it going to take to get you to buy today," is not what we need to be doing. We need to be solving problems. If I came to you today and said, "Hey, my family has been just raked over the coals with the flu this year," and you say, "What kind of antioxidant product are you taking to make your family, from an immune system perspective, more healthy?" "Well, we're not." "Well let me get you a sample of one. If it works out for you, great – I will show you where you can get it. If not, no big deal." This is pulling you out of the equation.

It's the same manner with income opportunities: I always approach people from a third party perspective – "Listen: I am working with one of the partners from one of the fastest growing companies out of Dallas,

Texas. Last time I was chatting with him, they told me to identify five or six people who are looking to create some additional income. I thought of you. If it can work out for you, I would love to sit down and run through some numbers with you; if it's something you might want to pursue, great! If not, no big deal."

The average personal invitation in network marketing is, "Hey, I started a new business; come take a look at it. I want to sit down and show you my deal." This is a big mistake! I have to teach this all the time – the average person getting started in this industry, especially if they are working initially within their warm market, is going to be shot down over and over again because those people know you! What is the likelihood of my little brother starting a business that is going to be a major success? I know my little brother – I changed his diapers – that kind of stuff! It is much more likely that you know someone, or meet someone, who is the founding partner of a new company. Whatever the case may be, whatever your verbiage is, I don't know, but I always do a third party invite. Even though, yes, I could answer any questions I have about it today, it's still the best way to go about it.

Then the last piece in that puzzle is that so often people do so much talking when they are inviting people to see a presentation that they have nothing to talk about if they land an appointment. I teach our folks that if you are going to sell anything, sell the appointment. Sell the appointment because you don't want – you don't need to fill them with every single bit of information right up front. Here's the reality: it doesn't matter what a person says or asks questions about, particularly from a business perspective. If they are not interested in developing an additional stream of income outside of whatever they are doing, then it doesn't matter what it is. We are never going to sit down and get to what it is, unless they have already identified themselves as someone that is looking to get into something like that.

So the bottom line is to pull yourself out of positions where you are taking the hit from rejection yourself because it not only will work better for you in the long run from a results perspective, but also from a self-image perspective. Does that make sense?

Q. What have been the biggest rewards for you from your networking activities?

A. I would say, without a doubt, the freedom to be a full-time dad and full-time husband. My commute on a daily basis is typically from upstairs, down the stairs, and into my home office; or getting into my car and driving to Starbucks to pick up lattes for my wife and me, then driving home. This level of freedom is tremendous! I am a night owl; I like to stay up late, and so I don't like to get up early. I know that many people in my neighborhood are getting up at six o'clock in the morning and driving sometimes an hour to work. They are living a life that I chose to not live; I chose to be an entrepreneur and do things differently.

This doesn't mean that I don't work hard. That would be a big misunderstanding. I work as hard as anybody in corporate America, especially in particular seasons, but I work on my own terms. That means that I've got a calendar and I am pretty good with it. If I put my son's basketball championship game in my calendar, guess what? There is nothing that is going to come in the way of that game! There's no boss to tell me that I have to stay late at work that day, right? So I have the freedom to do the things that I want to do, when I want to do them, and the income level that allows me

Ty Tribble

to not be concerned with what is happening on a day-to-day basis.

Here is what I mean by that: In a lot of ways, people think of those who make money as materialistic; that they always think and talk about money, especially where I live in the United States. I have been broke. When I was a kid, my mom and I had no money whatsoever. When you have no money and you are worried about how in the world you are going to squeeze $200 out of thin air to pay that bill in front of you, which is two weeks overdue, you are thinking a lot about money. Contrast that to when there is money. You don't even concern yourself when the bill comes in, because no bills come in that will make a big enough dent in your checking account for it to matter.

The reality is, when I am doing a presentation about my business, a big portion of what I am talking about is making money, so of course I am going to talk a lot about money. But it doesn't mean I am materialistic. Frankly, I spend less time today thinking about money, than I did when I was driving a used Ford Taurus and working 70 hours a week, scraping by with both my wife and I working.

Today one of the things that I love to see, that makes me the happiest, is that my wife is able to volunteer on a continual basis. She loves to volunteer for both of my kids' schools, so she is always off running around. People call her a stay at home mom, except she is never home, so I don't know where they get that idea. Between working out and volunteering at school, she is always running around doing something. For her to have the freedom to do the things she chooses to do is a big blessing. Are the cars nice? Absolutely – like I said, I've got the top down on the Porsche that

I earned from my company today. But frankly I could do without the Porsche as long as I had the time, freedom, and ability to spend quality time with my family when I choose to, and when they need me.

Q. What have been your biggest challenges?

A. My first five or ten years really, in the industry, was one big challenge. It had everything to do with – it was so many things – but mostly to do with the mentoring and coaching that I was getting at the time. The person was not concerned with my best interests; he was concerned with extracting as much money out of me as he could. When that changed, so did my business and my income level, and to be honest, my ability to make an impact on people's lives changed as well. One of the things that I am most proud of is just in the last five months, is that I have helped 30 people in my team earn BMW's through our company's compensation plan. I remember when I didn't have 30 people in my whole down line team. So, the struggle in the beginning is that you can work really, really hard and get no results. A lot of it has to do with maybe the timing or positioning of your company in particular, as well as having the wrong mentorship, and that can affect things when you can really get moving.

Today it is a blessing; our business is growing much faster than I can even keep track of and yet what is interesting is that I am putting in the same amount of effort as before. It's just the results that are different. There are a lot of reasons for this, but that is probably the main thing.

Q. How important are "direct response" marketing skills to attraction marketing or networking professionally? Are they complimentary, necessary, or something completely different?

A. Absolutely make a call to action. I go into this when I talk about how to craft a great blog post. Marketing overall, and the psychology of selling, is very interesting. Frankly it has not changed very much since the 1930's. We use different technology but the basics of it are still the same today.

I think it is vital to make sure that there is some reasoning and some real thought process put behind everything that you do online. For example, people might go start a blog because they know they need to have one, but they might not know what the purpose of their blog is in the first place. I think Mark Hoverson, as an example, is very good at having a purpose behind every single thing that he does. So he doesn't send an email out without having a very specific purpose. His email is not just content running around the Internet for no reason. I hardly even knew what a blog was when I started. As a matter of fact, back in 2003, if I told someone that I was blogging, they'd say "What's that?" Then they would look at me as if I had a third eye. So did I know what to do with the blog? No, but today is a completely different story.

So overall, yes: there has to be some very specific thought process put behind what you do in your business and how you spend your time. Are you spending eight hours a day tweeting on Twitter about nothing, in the hopes of developing a relationship with someone? Or are you systematically putting out tweets that drive people back to your blog, knowing full well that out of every 100 people that hit your blog you are getting five to ten opt-ins for your specific offer, right? Or two to three, whatever the number is – I have no idea; it can vary.

There's a big difference between that and just tweeting, blogging, and thinking, "I need to put a blog post because Ty said it's a great thing to do and it's going to build me business." Well, I think there has got to be some specific intent behind what you are doing online, not just going through the motions.

Then the biggest thing is when you have people you can call about your business, on your list of names. If you choose to write a blog post, tweet or update your Facebook profile instead of picking up the phone and calling those people, goodness gracious! You are missing the boat! The reality is that you should be doing those things that I talked about online while your prospects are sleeping.

If you are in the right company, the products, the timing and the opportunity today are too good to attempt to be learning an online skill set that you are not 100% ready to jump into, especially given this current economic situation. In other words, the opportunity is too good for you to spend five hours a day watching training videos. This is not productive; it's not making you money. So it's absolutely vital that there is a strong call to action in just about everything you do, and some real thought process and intent behind it.

Q. Is there anything else you want to share with an aspiring networker or attraction marketer?
A. I mean, I think that the biggest thing that people miss is consistency. This can apply directly to their blog, to social media, or to their overall network marketing business in terms of picking up the phone, making calls, and things of that nature.

Recently I saw that my blog was number 41 or 42 on the top 100 small business blogs online today. That's a huge statement, not just because it is me, which I am proud of. But also because of the reality that a "networking marketing/MLM" blog being among the top 50 small business blogs in the world, provides tremendous credibility for the industry as a whole. I did not become the "number one blogger" on the subject of network marketing by throwing up a blog post once every 34 days.

How did I do it? I became the top blogger in this field by making one to two blog posts a day over a significant time period. The consistency factor was a huge piece of that puzzle. So, consistency, consistency, consistency in everything that you do in this business will get you far. As you consistently work on things, you are going to get better at everything you do, and you know what? It takes practice! Everything you do takes practice; so don't feel like you are going to be a professional in network marketing when you just started six months ago, or twelve months ago, or eighteen months ago. I mean, there are people who have been at it for 20 years. When you hear them speak, you think, "Wow, I hope one day I can do that!" If they have been at it for 20 years, they better be that good!

Overall, I am just excited about the opportunity for people to get out, stretch their entrepreneurial wings, and build businesses of their own. To take control of their financial future and not let the economy, a boss, or someone else dictate what level of success they are going to attain in 2010, but take control of those reins themselves and go do it. In terms of leaving anything on the table, that's exactly what I would say!

BLOGGER AND SOCIAL MEDIA ENTREPRENEUR

SUMMARY

- People often don't simplify things enough
- Being with the right company and having the right mentorship makes all the difference
- Pitching your latest greatest deal all the time adds no value to anyone and gets annoying
- Rather than running around trying to pitch your deal to people, be a solutions provider
- With social media, don't talk about your business 24/7. Talk about cool stuff from life
- Attractive networkers provide people with great value, whether people choose to be in business with them, or not
- College is not very useful from an Internet marketing perspective. Things change too fast
- Personal development is vital. Be a student!
- Personal development, leadership and people skills developed through network marketing can serve you well in traditional businesses
- Be open to receiving value from others whether free or through good paid material
- If you are not open to buying from others, why would you expect people to be open to buying from you?
- Learn to lead in a way that has your follower's best interests at heart
- Balance online and offline activities
- You cannot build a network without building relationships with people
- Look for people to work with who have similar values to you
- Don't do so much talking when inviting people to see a presentation that you have nothing to talk about if you land an appointment
- It's absolutely vital that there is a strong call to action in just about everything you do and some real thought process and intent behind it

Ty Tribble

161

- The biggest thing that people miss is consistency. As you consistently work on things, you are going to get better at everything you do
- Take control of your financial future and don't let the economy, a boss, or someone else dictate what level of success you are going to attain this year

TY TRIBBLE'S RECOMMENDED RESOURCES
- *Crush It* – Gary Vaynerchuk
- *How to Win Friends and Influence People* – Dale Carnegie
- *The Power of Positive Thinking* – Dr. Norman Vincent Peale
- *The Magic of Thinking Big* – David Schwartz
- *How to Have Confidence and Power in Dealing with People* – Les Giblin
- *Magnetic Sponsoring* – Mike Dillard
- *MLM Traffic Formula II* – Mike Dillard
- *The Renegade Network Marketer* – Ann Sieg
- *The Renegade Professional* subscription – Mike Klingler and Ann Sieg

TY TRIBBLE'S RECOMMENDED RESOURCES ONLINE
http://50networkers.com/ty-tribble

NINE

It's all about connecting the dots, really. Knowing what you can add, what you can give, what you can contribute, what you can offer, before anything else.
Noel Wu, Personal Image & Wardrobe Consultant, Fashion Designer

Noel Wu is quite possibly connected to more famous people than anyone else I have ever met. His clients include celebrities, accomplished athletes, powerful professionals, U.S. politicians (including several presidents) and Fortune 500 CEOs.

Noel was born in Bali, Indonesia. His father was a successful entrepreneur. However, when Noel was nine, his father became very ill. His business partner abandoned them, taking everything and leaving Noel's father on his deathbed with all the debts of the business. When his father died, Noel's family quickly went from being wealthy to the poor house; living in a shack with a dirt floor and no running water. Noel had to start working at the age of nine. He came to the United States when he was around sixteen. As an immigrant teenager, Noel faced a strong culture shock living in southern California, and life in the U.S. was not as rosy as he had expected.

Although Noel finished college, he learned the most important things outside of formal education institutions.

Noel still had his father's entrepreneurial spirit and discovered he didn't fit in the standard job system. He didn't believe in the system, couldn't seem to hold down a job for long, and had student loans to pay back.

Things turned around when Noel met the owner of a large high-end custom clothing company. They talked, and hit it off very well. The man was scouting for someone entrepreneurial, so Noel came on board and went through their entire training program. During this time, Noel met a lot of the big players in the fashion industry – people like Donna Karen, Gianni Versace and Ralph Lauren. Noel travelled a lot, and quickly became the director of corporate sales. He created a program for this company as a corporate liaison and started talking to a lot of high-end and prominent clients. The relationships that Noel built while working for this company outlasted the company itself. The owner of the company retired at ninety-two, the company was sold to the wrong buyer, and a sixty-three year old successful company went bankrupt over the next seven years.

Noel had been with the company for ten years, and had built strong relationships with his clients. They all knew Noel as their source, so when the company folded, it was an easy transition for Noel to start his own company and bring his clients into it.
Noel had hit the ground running, and was now full swing into his new solo entrepreneurial venture.

In the twelve years since he formed his own company, Noel's unique position working with powerful and successful people grew even more through referrals and the application of an incentive program that his clients embraced.

Noel has expanded his role beyond the exclusive clothing industry to focus on helping individuals with their self-

PERSONAL IMAGE AND WARDROBE CONSULTANT

image and self-confidence in their personal and professional lives.

Q. You were talking about the corporate training where you were introduced to the big players like Donna Karen and all the others. Is networking very important in that particular industry – who you know and who you get introduced to?

A. Yes, absolutely! You have to remember: my responsibility was the director of corporate sales. I handled the high, prominent clients for the company so I was the "go to" guy. I was strictly the guy who was in charge of the program and I started the program, so all the clients that I dealt with mostly knew the company through me. So to those clients, I was the company. They never had to come anywhere to deal with the company because when they wanted anything, I would travel across the country. I went to see them in the comfort of their office or their home. The business is really very exclusive. It's a tight industry and not a very big one, so business really grew from word of mouth. I would get referrals from clients who are happy and satisfied with my service. Almost every single time I see a client they will say, "I have a colleague of mine," or, "So-and-so would need your service; would you please give them a call and get in touch with them?"

> *"...a personalized greeting card. I found that it's more effective than corporate marketing and all this multi-billion dollar marketing."*

The only thing we did as far as marketing efforts for the business was to send out greeting cards every year. That's all – a personalized greeting card. I found that

NOEL WU

it's more effective than corporate marketing and all this multi-billion dollar marketing.

Q. Would you say that it was when you actually started with this particular company that you were introduced to networking, or did you have a concept of networking before that?

A. I had a concept – that's how I created that corporate liaison pilot program with the company. The secret of the program was incentivizing the existing clients so that they would grow the business for us. I would come up with a special bonus or program for those who would refer their colleagues, family or friends – if they are satisfied with our service and product. It worked very, very well because they didn't need to worry about anything else. All they needed to do was tell their friends, and if their friends mentioned their name, they automatically received a credit in their account for the referral.

> *"...but you have to remember: the only reason it worked is because of the service and product that the clients received from me to begin with."*

Q. How long were you involved in networking or attraction marketing before you actually started to see some tangible results for your business?

A. It was almost instant. Within a week! Just as soon as I started that program, it caught on like a wild fire. It was such a success that I would do it all over again. It was very satisfying to see the results, but you have to remember: the only reason it worked is because of the service and product that the clients received from me to begin with. If they did not receive anything or they did not get the impression of satisfaction, then it never would have happened.

Q. I actually met you at a conference. Do you go to many conferences and events like the one I met you at?

A. I always believed in getting yourself out there, getting yourself connected. A good friend of mine, you probably know who he is – Brian Tracy, said something which is common to any larger than life successful individual… "It's all about connecting the dots."

What I mean by connecting the dots is really your networking activities, your effort of planting the seeds out there, sowing the seeds with no reservation. You are almost doing it like a "paying it forward" type of thing. It's almost pro-bono a lot of times. It's almost like you go into any setting, situation, or any relationship in life; whether it's personal or professional, you always see yourself as a "value added" type of person rather than taking away value from it.

If you just go into any setting with that mindset, thinking, "How can I be of value to you, to the group, or to whatever it is? How can I add? How can I give? How can I contribute?" You never go in with the mindset thinking, "What's in it for me? What can I get out of it?" If you go in it like that you will never get anywhere. The majority of people go everywhere thinking, "What's in it for me?" first. If they don't see anything in it for them, they are not interested. They get turned off, leave, and that's the problem. That's why no one gets anywhere in their life quickly, successfully; it's because they think in this scarcity mind set.

You have to think in an abundance mindset in order for you to really gain an inch in life, because the more abundance you create, the more abundance follows. Unfortunately we are all complacent with our own life

NOEL WU

and our greed that we don't see something as obvious as that. It's kind of sad in a way.

So the moral of the story I am telling about connecting the dots, that's the whole point. It has a lot to do with the things I just said. You have to know how to connect the dots. Everybody has the dots, but they just don't know how to connect them. They don't know how to maneuver, where to go first, and how to add value to it. So those dots, a lot of times, in everybody's life are just wasted as resources for themselves.

But what I mean by dots; every individual you meet is a dot. You are a dot. I am a dot. You see what I mean? If you see the value you can add, you can contribute. If you see how I can be a value to whatever setting you know, and you know that it would be beneficial, and you put me as a dot into that setting and it starts just adding tremendous value in that setting. Guess what kind of benefit will come out? It will come out and it will go back to you because you are the one that connected the dots.

Q. **So you are saying that connecting the dots, that seeking to give value to everyone you meet, is what makes an attractive networker?**

A. It's what makes everybody successful, not only in networking. I am serious; it's just a principle of life. That's the bottom line. It's all about connecting the dots. You take every successful person and they will give you exactly the same answer. They will say, "I couldn't have done it myself; there's no way I could have done it by myself." There are other people behind them or around them that make things happen for them along the way to get to where they are today. Behind every successful individual, there is a very powerful team, meaning there's a very powerful network behind them.

Q. **That's the positive side of networking, what you should do. Is there any particular mistakes people make that you would say are unforgiveable in networking?**

A. Absolutely! Like I just said earlier, you cannot think scarcity. If you go into networking with a mentality of thinking that you are going to get something out of it, and thinking what's in it for you, or going in with your greedy attitude, as a person that's going to become detrimental to you. You can't fool people who know how to connect the dots, we will sense it immediately if it's not genuine.

You have to be genuine. You go in with no agenda whatsoever. Like the way I walked into that conference in Las Vegas where we met. No agenda whatsoever; I was not planning to go; I didn't even want to go at that time because my schedule was just too full. However, I decided to go because of a high recommendation, and a video they showed me. I asked my assistant to set up a time and we made that event. I was glad that I did – I didn't plan to be on stage at that event but I was invited on stage. That's how it is. I just went to go, observe, and see who I might run into, see what I could do for the group, what I could offer, what I could contribute. So you can't just go in thinking, "If there's no benefit for me I don't belong there." That's thinking scarcity. You will never get anywhere.

Q. **What kind of things have you done consciously to improve your networking skills?**

A. In a way it is simple, but not as simple as everybody thinks. Again, the most important thing is your mindset, your mentality. You have to be an open-minded person to walk into any setting like a sponge so you can really absorb a lot of good things and information. A lot of times people really guard themselves, thinking, "You know what? I know enough, I don't really need to learn this anymore." That's when it becomes stagnant and very detrimental for themselves. When you build that kind of wall, yes it's true that you block the bad guys, or the bad things, from coming into your life. But think about what else you have blocked out too. You have also blocked out a lot of good things that could be coming into your life by doing that. So the bottom line is you have to just go in it with an open mind, being a quick learner and just observe and adapt.

When you say nothing it doesn't mean that you don't know anything. So I tend to do that. I don't pretend that I know everything. As a matter of fact, I pretend that I don't know anything. People tend to be more receptive of you when you show your eagerness, to learn from them, and to get to know them. So I think the approach of networking is really just that humility goes a long way, being humble, and at the same time being professional, being an open-minded person. You don't have to be the life of the party. Seriously, you don't. I have had very, very pleasant results with those kinds of traits.

Q. **Do you have any particular recommended training resources, books, classes, anything like that which come to mind?**

A. The first thing you have to have is that open mentality and mindset. If you don't have it, you need to nurture and nourish it first before you do anything else. Overcoming your own misconceptions is the hardest thing to learn. So the best thing to do is to start learning from the people who have achieved larger-than-life kind of success. I can testify with conviction, that any of these guys – Tony Robins, Brian Tracy, Eben Pagan, and

Brendon Burchard – are not any smarter or more intelligent. What sets them apart is their visionary mentality. They have this vision, and they have developed the resources to move forward on it, they know how to act on it. Any of us are capable of doing the same thing, so the best thing to begin with is to train yourself with the right mindset.

I would say the best book to read is Napoleon Hill's, *Think and Grow Rich*. Another highly recommended book for people who have yet to form their mindset and set themselves in a winning mentality is *The Tipping Point* by Malcolm Gladwell. Reading just these two books will put you ahead of many people out there. And you will be ready to go into any networking event and setting and know how to talk, and know how to carry yourself.

Q. Online networking, offline networking: is one better than the other, do you need both, or is it a matter of personal style and skills?

A. Both types of networking are good, but it's just as important that you network in the right places and to the right crowd that is compatible with your beliefs and values. As far as online networking, my assistant does this on my behalf. I believe social media is catching on like a wildfire now. The online thing is fairly new to me because I am old school, but I do have people on my team that handle the technological side of social media and business automation. As a team, we do a lot of networking efforts focused on expanding our reach and our horizon.

The power and technology of the Internet makes it possible for someone like me to reach out to a lot broader audience that I didn't even expect or dream to reach out to 10 or 15 years ago. I realized the potential

NOEL WU

of me touching more lives and helping more people out there, is not only possible, but it is now a reality. This empowers me to set a goal of touching one million souls in ten years or less with the program and framework that I am setting up.

Q. What have been the biggest rewards for you from your networking activities?

A. Here's an example of a reward from the Las Vegas event I just mentioned. I was able to touch many lives there in a very special way by my presentation and interaction with everybody there in the group. Then after the event, many kept in touch. Many came on board and joined the group I started in the online community. I think that's the biggest reward; when you know people appreciate your presence and people appreciate your contribution and the value that you added. That's how you gain people into your network and they become not just another network member, but friends and fans, who are ready to help you anytime you need their support.

Q. What have been your biggest challenges?

A. The biggest challenge is coming across people who have the wrong mindset; people who get into networking thinking only what they can get out of it. I don't have the time to educate those who think this way, so when I notice or identify people who think they can always take and never offer anything, I move on.

Q. Is there anything else you want to share with an aspiring networker or attraction marketer?

A. Again, I would say – I could never say it enough – it's all about connecting the dots, really. It's all about knowing what you can add, what you can give, what you can contribute, what you can offer, before anything else.

What steps do successful people take? Why do only a very small percentage achieve "larger-than-life" kind of success? The rest are just living their life in mediocrity, thinking of the old advice of "Go out and get your college education, get your degree, go get a corporate job, climb the corporate ladder, save your money, invest wisely, and then retire." That advice is detrimental. It's like they condition, almost brainwash, everybody. They believe in the system and that's the way life should be, and that it is normal for people to go through life that way. People look around them and they see "Oh, okay, so-and-so, my neighbors, my friends, my family live their lives the way they do, and I am not so far apart from them, so this is normal. I am fine. I will be okay." That's why you see a lot of people, when they reach seventy, often they worry about getting a second job, and you find them at Wal-Mart greeting customers or working at McDonalds. That's just very sad. That's the broken American dream. People live beyond their means, people live on the standard and mindset of others based on the mediocrity that they see around them.

I have a comment about a popular spin on the law of attraction that I believe is very misleading. While the law of attraction has worked from the beginning of time, Brian Tracy made attraction marketing popular in the professional world. But a film based on the book, The Secret, misled people about a key point in the law of attraction. The film seemed to show that if you believe in the law of attraction you don't need to do anything. You just need to have positive thoughts and all of a sudden blessings will fall out of the sky like magic. That's not true. It will never happen that way.

NOEL WU

But the other half of the truth is that the law of attraction works only if you put your effort into it, only if you are willing to go through the uncomfortable times, only if you are willing to endure trouble. If you are willing to set sail with a plan of action and

> *"...the successful are willing to fail many, many times before they succeed once. The unsuccessful are not willing to fail even once."*

are putting that plan into action. You work and succeed, and if you don't succeed you rework your plan or come up with a new one. So basically what sets the unsuccessful and the successful apart is that the successful are willing to fail many, many times before they succeed once. The unsuccessful are not willing to fail even once. If they fail once they think it's not their cup of tea. That's why so few people truly succeed.

SUMMARY

- Be genuine
- Being seen as the "Go-To" person for your clients builds relationships and can encourage referrals
- If you already provide excellent service or products, you can incentivize referrals
- A personalized greeting card can be a very effective marketing tool
- Behind every successful individual is a very powerful team or network
- Connecting people to other people who add value is like connecting the dots. This is vital to success
- Don't think only of what you can get out of an event or a relationship. Think of what you can give

PERSONAL IMAGE AND WARDROBE CONSULTANT

- Be open to learning from others. Don't be a know-it-all
- What sets the unsuccessful and the successful apart is that the successful are willing to fail many, many times before they succeed once

NOEL WU'S RECOMMENDED RESOURCES
- *Think and Grow Rich* – Napoleon Hill
- *The Tipping Point* – Malcolm Gladwell

NOEL WU'S RECOMMENDED RESOURCES ONLINE
http://50networkers.com/noel-wu

NOEL WU

TEN

B eing an entrepreneur is a
team sport.
**Michael Wilson, Online Business
and Marketing Strategist**

Michael Wilson has had an entrepreneurial spirit from a young age and formed his first business, a painting company, while in high school. He kept the business going to pay for college.

Michael was raised in Wichita, Kansas. He studied chemistry at Rockhurst University in Kansas City, earning a B.S. in chemistry. According to Michael, the main thing that people learn in college is how to think, and he was no exception in this regard. Michael used this experience to learn investigative thinking and problem-solving skills. Michael raised his family in Kansas City during a successful twenty year career in the corporate world, starting with chemistry, and moving into the fields of sales and marketing. Michael returned to his entrepreneur beginning about six years ago, focusing on networking and online marketing. Michael is a full-time coach and consultant for all types of businesses – brick and mortar, traditional businesses, purely online business, MLM, etc. – focusing on their online marketing strategies or their marketing strategies in general. Currently, Michael lives in Virginia and works with people from around the world.

MICHAEL WILSON

Q. How long were you involved in networking or attraction marketing before you actually started to see some tangible results for your business?

A. We called network marketing "Sheep Dipping" back when I started with it. I was fully dipped in all the old style methods of sales and marketing that have been in vogue for the last few decades when I joined my first company. I was really solid on these methods, but simply was not successful using them, even though I liked the company and the financial product. To me it felt like how you feel when you are sold defective goods. You were told one thing and something entirely different was delivered. I went through all these experiences and soured on it quickly. I had a very successful corporate career and was running my own business. I am used to success, and this wasn't success. It didn't feel right or work right, and it wasn't returning anything. I stopped working for this company in that way, but I am actually still involved with the same company today.

> *"... I never would have been successful in network marketing had I not dove into different types of techniques."*

My first success with network marketing was a year and a half later, when I really started working attraction marketing techniques. That was my first introduction to online marketing and network marketing philosophies that made any amount of sense.

I firmly believe that I never would have been successful in network marketing had I not dove into different types of techniques. Attraction marketing is one of them. I teach attraction marketing and a lot of its techniques are extremely valid. I also teach direct-response

ONLINE BUSINESS AND MARKETING STRATEGIST

marketing; I think those are extremely valid as well. They peacefully coexist, it's not one or the other, it's a whole bag of tools that all work. Had I not gotten into that, I think the clock would have just kept ticking. I either would have gone broke, gone nuts, or gone back to get a job if I had stayed with network marketing the way that I was doing it.

I believe using attraction marketing and doing on-line marketing "Renegade community" style, takes a while to actually see some success. It's different than just dollars, and I think that it takes a number of weeks and months to really build something – three to six months – of pretty significant time investment to build something that is returning what attraction marketing should return. Something that is connecting you with the prospects, customers and potential customers who are interested in what you have to offer that you can have a connection with. That's about how long it took me. I went very deep into attraction marketing and in the middle of that I probably changed my business focus to end up where I am at today, which is actually teaching a lot of these principles.

Q. Were there any significant milestones or turning points along the way?

A. The first big turning point was finding Ann Sieg's books, *The 7 Great Lies of Network Marketing* and *The Renegade Network Marketer*. They were the first things that I read on the topic that made any sense to me, and which led to all of the other things that I did eight months later. I was in touch with Ann's group but wasn't getting it until I joined her *Renegade Breakthrough Mentoring Program*. I carefully thought through all the aspects of doing the program in April 2009, from commitment to cost, and went for it. It was a significant turning point, because it introduced me to not just the ideas that I needed to hear, the skills that I needed to learn and the higher level of information that I needed to see, but it introduced me to the community, to a group of like-minded people. That was an ignition point for me.

One of my biggest "Ah ha!" moments from that community was learning that business, especially as entrepreneurs, is a team sport. You don't do it alone. The faster you learn to find the right people, associate with the right people, and figure out how you can help them; the faster you are going to be working with something larger than, and other than, yourself; and the faster you are going to progress. This was a big "Ah ha!" moment and it came fairly early on in the Renegade Breakthrough Mentoring community.

Q. What makes the difference between an attractive networker, a boring networker and an irritating networker?

A. That's funny because I think they are all the same person at different stages. There's a riddle – what's that riddle? What animal walks on four legs, then two legs, then three legs? The riddle of the Sphinx!

When I first started my network marketing company, they told me how to do things and I did them. I am results oriented and an achiever, so I did what I was told. I was irritating as hell because that's what those tactics teach you; that's what happens when you use those tactics. You become irritating and you just irritate people normally. It's "spammy", it's irritating, it's pushy, and I was. I was an irritating marketer. I was crawling like a baby.

Then I became a boring marketer because I learned different ways to market. I was trying to add value, to be beneficial; but that was all I could do. I wasn't being irritating anymore, but I was boring. I use several coaches. Some time ago, one of my coaches said, "Michael, I am just going to be honest with you. I see what you are trying to do here with what you have written, but you are just boring!" Which is funny because it was right in the middle of this stage, and he said, "I know you and you are not boring so quit trying to be boring here". I think that boring marketing is just a phase that a lot of people go through.

It's a challenge to get up to the attractive level, the last level in the series. The attractive level is when you have learned to add value; you've learned to do it in a personal way, an entertaining way, and a non-pushy way. You've learned to be a resource and to help people solve their problems. You've learned to focus on others and people are attracted to that.

There are a lot of leadership qualities in being an attractive marketer. I think that's where people get to as they mature in their marketing. It's not that some people choose to be irritating or boring. Well, some people may choose to be irritating, but if you go back in the history of most people who become attractive marketers, they will tell you stories of when they were irritating or boring at one time or another.

This shows that there is hope for all of us, no matter which stage we are currently at, in our journey towards becoming an attractive marketer.

Q. What kind of things have you done consciously to improve your networking skills?
A. First and foremost – and this is actually another "Ah ha!" moment for my breakthrough – becoming valuable as a collaboration partner, becoming valuable in somebody else's network is a skill that you can learn.

MICHAEL WILSON

It's something that is teachable, it's learnable, and so knowing it – and then working towards, is important.

The reason I say it this way is because you can go out and try to meet a bunch of people, but that is kind of like building a list on Twitter with an automated system. It can almost be on the irritating end of things. Real networking skills are measured by the value brought to others.

There are a couple of ways to do this. One of them is to just educate yourself – and that's something that I did. I spent a lot of time and money on education. In fact, I spent well over the average amount of money learning skills. For example, *Coaching Cognition* teaches excellent interpersonal skills and consultative selling skills.

> *"Real networking skills are measured by the value brought to others."*

These are important skills that help with networking, help to make you valuable, and help enable you to recognize how you can help somebody else. It's only when you start to become valuable to other people that you find yourself attracting other opportunities. This is the heart of networking. If you don't bring some value into a relationship, there can't be any reciprocity there, because you don't have anything to give yet.

Another conscious thing that I did, and am still active in, was joining a book club for marketing, entrepreneurship and personal improvement. The types of books that we read are mainly personal development, designed for somebody in business for themselves.

A real obvious way to network, that people miss a lot, is go to the places and hang out with the people that

ONLINE BUSINESS AND MARKETING STRATEGIST

you want to be like. Now there's a skill to this. You've got to go places. It's not as easy as just buying a ticket. You can travel, go to a meeting, and not get anything out of it, or you can make connections, learn things, teach things, and network. You can build a valuable piece of your network and more importantly, become a valuable piece in someone else's network.

Q. Do you have any particular recommended training resources, books, classes, anything like that which come to mind?

A. There are the standard ones *Think and Grow Rich* and *Rich Dad, Poor Dad*. For the entrepreneur who is in business to make money, not as a hobby, and wants to do better, I would also recommend Dan Kennedy's *"NO B.S."* series, especially *NO B.S. Business Success*. Almost all of Dan's work resonates with me, and I probably own double digits of his material. There is an aspect of direct response, urgency and cause and effect that is helpful to any entrepreneur.

A book that has become popular more recently is *The 4-Hour Work Week* by Timothy Ferris. This book is down and dirty; you can implement some of the ideas, but it will also change your mindset. In our community – the Renegade community, entrepreneur communities, and business communities – this book is gaining popularity and it spoke to me as well. I read it in one sitting and changed some things in my business plan based on it.

One book that's kind of off the beaten path is called *The Talent Code*. I just read it not too long ago. We used it for personal improvement – but it's really about how people learn and leap frog in learning; making quantum leaps in skill levels, jobs, performance or anything. Then for training courses, I would say a couple of things. Obviously I am big into Renegade. I did Ann Sieg's series, *The Renegade Professional, Renegade Breakthrough Mentoring Program*. I was a founding member in *PBN* (Professional, Business & Non-profit). I was in the pilot group in the *Coaching Cognition* program, went all the way through that training, graduated, and became a contributor. I became a *Renegade Super Guide* trainer. Outside of this there were a variety of "fill in the gap" types of things that I also did in terms of training courses.

> *"Get a coach. Get a couple... Don't be afraid to get another one and don't be afraid to trade out the one you've got if he's not working for you."*

The biggest of those was a personal development and coaching program combined. I would recommend this to anybody who wants to get serious about being a long-term successful business owner and entrepreneur. Look inside.

Personal development is a big deal. I was hesitant to jump into it because, to be honest, I really didn't think it had that much to do with business. But I found it to be a big catalyst. It was the most expensive, single in depth training course that I have ever taken. Some of my goals were business obviously, but it focused primarily on personal development.

This leads me to the last thing – and this is absolutely the biggest thing: Get a coach. Get a couple! If you can only afford one coach, then pick your highest priority and get a coach. If you can't afford a coach, get a peer coach; trade some coaching. If you can't afford any of that and you don't know anybody, get a mentor.

ONLINE BUSINESS AND MARKETING STRATEGIST

Don't be afraid to get another one and don't be afraid to trade out the one you've got if he's not working for you. But having that personal guidance, interaction, and safe haven for whatever needs to come out that day is probably top on the list, or darn close to it for important things and business success.

Q. Are there any particular mistakes people make that are unforgivable in networking?

A. People make some of their biggest mistakes in the "irritating" phase of their development, but most of those things are not unforgivable, and they grow through and out of them.

Unethical behavior is one thing, or error, that people do that is as close to unforgivable as you can get. It can be a fatal flaw in terms of fatal for your business. Simply put; you rip somebody off; you just don't deliver. There are all sorts of ways people think about ethical and unethical behavior. I am on the end of the scale where I try to avoid even the appearance of impropriety. I think that's the end of the scale to act on; that's the way you need to run your business because your single greatest asset is your own reputation and credibility; your name. It's especially true for network marketers and online marketers, independent, individual business owners because done well, you are branding yourself. If you ruin your name or your credibility, then you have ruined your entire brand. That's as close to fatal as you can get.

Especially early on, when you are just starting out and you are hungry, you want money so badly you can be tempted to overpromise; to say or do things that you can't deliver on. It is tempting to be unethical. Don't do it! It is just not worth it. If you avoid even the appearance of impropriety, then you can sleep at night

Michael Wilson

and you've done well. If you make decisions that way, you not only don't risk your reputation, you build your reputation.

Q. Let's say I have just started with my brand new network marketing business last week, so I am kind of at the pre-irritating stage. I could go down the irritating path and I feel like I don't really have any value to offer yet. I barely understand my own company. How do you actually provide real value and be ethical? How do you pick yourself up by your own boot straps?

A. That's a good question and that's a question that a lot of people in that stage struggle with. In fact, I would venture to say that almost everybody struggles with that. There are two questions there: Ethics and value.

How do you make sure that you maintain ethical behavior? That's easy: you do what you say you are going to do when you say you are going to do it. You deliver on your word, on your promise. So sometimes it's tempting to overpromise and that's just something that you just have to keep in mind. Even if I don't have as much to offer as I will later, then I am only going to sell you what I can deliver.

Being true to your word is a good way to do business. It is fundamental and always must be adhered to, in good times and in bad. In the beginning it appears to be bad times, because the person is struggling with a different concept, thinking "I can't determine or decide what I have that is valuable." Every single person, 100% of people, do have something of value.

Most people have many things of value. To say that I don't have anything of value because I am just starting out is really better worded as, "I have not yet discovered what value I can offer because I am just starting out."

Each individual has some value, they just haven't recognized it and more clearly they haven't recognized it in a business environment. Usually, people are trying to be valuable in the same way that they see somebody else operating, who is already seen as valuable. They may not have those same skills; they may have a different set of skills. They may not have the experiences that person is offering as value; they have other experiences.

Usually the solution to that lies in the changing of perspective, and more in discovering an innate value rather than creating it. Find a core skill set that can be built into business value that can be offered to somebody else. The first steps are usually in discovering it, and then optimizing it or then putting it into a business perspective.

Q. It can certainly be hard when you first start out to see how you can get beyond a "me too" kind of perspective.
A. I tell my clients a couple things. First, nearly every single person has this challenge and goes through this, so you are not alone. I did, and sometimes I still do regularly. If you are going into a new area, you are going to go through that stage again. It's easier because you have been through the exercise before, but the first time through you don't have any landmarks.

People have been there before. Almost all of the people that I work with that are in the "beginner" stage of marketing, even some intermediate marketers, the very first thing we spend time on is identifying their niche. Most people, including myself and many oth-

MICHAEL WILSON

ers, have changed their niche – or have even changed it a couple times. They thought they were good at, or wanted to do, or wanted to provide value in, a certain area – and the fact of the matter is they were uniquely qualified to add value in a different area. It made them a lot happier when they figured this out.

Q. Online networking, offline networking: is one better than the other, do you need both, or is it a matter of personal style and skills?

A. I am a proponent of a balanced, optimized marketing strategy, so that almost always includes online and offline, new technology and old school. There's still not really a replacement for a handshake online. There's not really a good replacement for a phone call. So that's one aspect about balance.

Another aspect of balance is determined by what you are selling. Are you selling a service? Are you selling a product? What kind of service or product? Is it inexpensive or are you asking somebody to put a lot of money into it? You've got to match and balance that with what you are trying to do and the market that you are trying to do it in.

Sometimes offline methods actually work significantly better than online, sometimes it's the other way around. In some extreme examples, you can get by just fine with all of one or all of the other, but in most cases, for most people, it's picking some mix that fits their skills and their marketplace and their business, their product. It's usually a mix of those things that ends up being the strongest package that the person does. You hit on all the points; it's business, it's product, it's market, it's online, it's offline, multiple tools, and it's also individual personal preference.

In marketing, a lot of times I talk to my clients or I am giving presentations and I talk about how you touch people seven times, seven ways. There's nothing magical about that, but it does bring home the point that dealing with people multiple times and in multiple ways is usually the most effective.

Q. How do you attract quality people into your network who might be good power partners, peer advisors or joint venture partners? People you can trust your referrals to, or people who might refer others to you?

A. Do good work, do due diligence, and test them out! Do good work and make yourself known through your ethical work. Be active. For example, if you want to attract people you are interested in collaborating with, you have to have something of value to them. It takes a little while to build a name, but the better you do that, the more you will be a valued partner or supplier to a customer, or partner to collaborator, and on and on. Then make yourself known. If you are trying to get customers, you've got to tell people you are trying to get customers. You've got to promote yourself, put yourself out there. Once you get them, whether its customer, collaborator or partner, you have to filter those.

Not everybody that finds you is going to be an ideal customer or collaborator for you, even if you are hungry and don't have a lot of business. Sometimes it's not going to be a win-win, a good match, or a fit for your goals. But when you do find them, the ones that are passing those filters, and you pass their filters – obviously it's reciprocal – then do your due diligence. Start small. As you go along, and you do good work together, you build confidence.

You also build credibility with multiple people through

MICHAEL WILSON

referrals. I don't always use the person's service before I refer others to them, but I always do an appropriate level of due diligence before I refer somebody over to a service, company or an individual. I need to know them, I need to see their work, and if it's something that I do use oftentimes I will test it out and I will just hire them. If you want to partner with somebody and work with them and they sell something that you use, go buy it. That gets their attention, but it also gives you a lot more information.

Q. **Does letting go of any emotional expectation of a sale, or personal agenda from a networking interaction, free you to have a more successful interaction?**

A. I would say letting go of the emotional demand that you put on yourself, or need to make that sale, absolutely does. But I would say that people should have the expectation of success. It comes out in your demeanor, in your voice. If you are in sales, you should have the expectation of a sale because that's the mindset that attracts sales and attracts success. When it becomes wound up with a need to have that sale, or that there's not ever going to be another one, that type of expectation does work against you, whereas a positive expectation of success, that's almost a lifestyle.

Q. **As a follow up from that, when you go into a networking interaction with someone, do you have a personal agenda? Or do you try to figure out what their needs are, what yours are, and if there is a match there without really having an agenda?**

A. As far as a personal agenda goes, it would depend on what stage your business is in. If you have a clear idea of what your core focus is, and have the discipline to not deviate from it, then that is your underlying agenda.

If you are just starting out or don't know what your core focus is yet, you might do projects that, in hindsight you think, "Wow, I am never going to use that again. We have created something that we are never going to sell and not going to use in my business and it's just outside of where my core focus is." At the time, perhaps you couldn't see that, but you learned something from it, and you gained something from the experience, hopefully something good – but you will only be able to see that in hindsight.

As you develop a very well established core focus, you know exactly what it is, you are absolutely filtering, and you are looking to make sure that you don't waste your time or the other person's time. It's respectful to them and it's respectful to you. But if it is in your area, and it's starting to pass through those filters, then being very much in tune with how you can bring value, and help the other person reach their goals – this is a key to success in that collaboration.

So there are two things: One is to make sure that it's going to be a win for you, and that it falls in your core focus. Otherwise you are not even going to be able to give it your best effort and it won't be a win for you; long term. So that's kind of a filtering for self-preservation, efficiency, and effectiveness.

Two: When it does pass that filter, then you absolutely have to make sure that you don't bring an agenda. Instead, you bring an open mind. "I am willing to do this, am open-minded about how it's going to be done, and am going to collaborate with these people. As we go forward, I want it to be more and more obvious that this is a good collaboration; that I can bring value – enough value that it's obvious to them that I am helping them reach their goals." And it should be reciprocal. It should be obvious that they are helping you reach your goals too. So once you get into that collaboration environment then it's not about you, it's about the bigger picture. That's the road to success, in my personal opinion.

Q. What have been the biggest rewards for you from your networking activities?

A. My biggest rewards have to do with the people that I have met and the people that I interact with today. Don't get me wrong. I had a long career and I worked for superb companies; some of the largest companies in the world. They attracted very high quality people. I am not making a comparison and demeaning anybody, but I would sometimes call it "trading up." I traded up like getting a newer or better car. That's how I feel about the groups of people I have been able to meet and interact with in this business that have the entrepreneurial mindset. I like to interact with people that are of this mindset and share my own philosophy and goals. You try to find and attract people like that. Viola, you look up one day and you are in a room full of people like that.

Q. What have been your biggest challenges?

A. To keep on doing things that did not appear to be returning results. I wasn't blessed with a lot of patience. I like to see cause and effect in things. Starting out, I didn't see the results I wanted, especially financial. Of all the areas where I like to do something and see some returns from it, the financial arena is the biggest one. It was a struggle when the revenue was slower and that period lasted a heck of a lot longer than I was used to. I was resolved to keep doing things that I know I liked, that intellectually are right, and that my heart says are right, telling myself: "I know I am pointed in the right direction, but I am not yet getting the returns. I am not yet getting the credibility. I am not yet attracting prospects. I am not yet earning the money that I want to. But I am going to get up tomorrow and I am going to do it all over again." This has probably been the biggest challenge.

Q. **How important are "direct response" marketing skills to attraction marketing or networking professionally? Are they complimentary, necessary, or something completely different?**

A. I'm going to say that they are somewhere in between the complimentary and necessary range. They are absolutely complimentary. It's an approach; it's a way of doing things. There are individuals who have met their goals – whether it's making money, building a business, attracting prospects, making friends, or whatever – they have met their goals and built their business using just one method and that's true for all of the major methods. There are some people, who have built an entire business with Myspace, or with social marketing on Facebook, or their biggest prospecting tool is Twitter, or a blog, or whatever and they only do that one thing. There are some people that do it all with PPC (Pay-Per-Click advertising). So I don't think there is anything that is necessary; it has to be within the individual.

Most people however, excel with a couple of key points and key tools: important things like marketing their business themselves, their skills, their goals, and they get good at those things. For a lot of people, direct response marketing is a faster road to success. It is usually easier to track. It is also measurable, so it's easier to adjust and things like that. There are some people that only use attraction marketing tools and they do just fine, they find ways to make that work for them. But those two particular things, those two

MICHAEL WILSON

approaches, methodologies, strategies if you will – are complimentary.

Q. Is there anything else you want to share with an aspiring networker or attraction marketer?

A. I will paraphrase a quote from Calvin Coolidge – it's about persistence and the power of persistence: "Nothing in the world can take the place of persistence. Talent will not, genius will not, education will not. Persistence and determination alone are omnipotent." So I always leave people with persistence – if you get up in the morning and it seems hopeless, check your meter. If you really want what it is that you are going after, then go ahead and get up and do it all again. So if that commitment is there, then it's persistence that is going to see you through and is going to carry the day.

SUMMARY

- Your single greatest asset is your own reputation and credibility, your name
- Don't overpromise; don't say or do things that you can't deliver on
- Co-operation and collaboration are important – being an entrepreneur is a team sport
- Real networking skills are measured by the value brought to others
- Not everybody that finds you is going to be an ideal customer or collaborator for you – sometimes it's not going to be a win-win
- Do good work, do due diligence, and test people out as you start working together
- Most people go through irritating and boring stages as they develop into an attractive marketer
- Keep learning and growing, there is hope
- If you think you have nothing of value to offer, this is not uncommon. You have not yet discov-

ONLINE BUSINESS AND MARKETING STRATEGIST

ered your innate value from your unique skills and experiences yet
- Get a coach!
- Don't be afraid to get another coach, and don't be afraid to trade out the one you got if they are not working for you
- If you can only afford one coach, then pick your highest priority and get a coach for that
- Attraction marketing and direct-response marketing both have extremely valid techniques. It's not one or the other
- Nothing in the world can take the place of persistence

Michael Wilson's recommended resources
- *NO B.S. Business Success*– Dan Kennedy
- The *"NO B.S."* series – Dan Kennedy
- *The 4-Hour Work Week* – Timothy Ferris
- *The Talent Code* – Daniel Coyle
- *The Renegade Professional* subscription– Ann Sieg and Mike Klingler
- *Renegade Breakthrough Mentoring Program*
- *PBN* (Professionals, Businesses & Non-Profits)
- *Coaching Cognition*
- *Think and Grow Rich* – Napoleon Hill
- *Rich Dad, Poor Dad* – Robert Kiyosaki
- Get a good coach, or a couple of coaches

Michael Wilson's recommended resources online
http://50Networkers.com/michael-wilson

Michael Wilson

About the Author

Rob Christensen comes from a profession-al/technical background, being a successful senior database consultant.

After the world shook in September 2001 while he had taken a year off to pursue oth-er interests, Rob found it difficult to re-establish profes-sional network connections.

In 2008 Rob came across the concept of attraction market-ing. Not knowing where to start, and having made some initial mistakes, Rob learned a great deal from some of the better known names in this field. He has spent a lot of time on personal development and graduated with the first class from Barbara Silva's *Coaching Cognition* program.

Rob decided to make the quantum leap to a whole new level in personal and professional development. He is personally interviewing 50 attraction marketing and net-working professionals to find out what works and what doesn't, hear where people have come from and where they are now – redefining what is possible. Rob can be reached at:

    eMail: rob@50interviews.com
    Facebook: http://50Networkers.com/facebook
    Twitter: @RobCoach
    Coaching: http://50Networkers.com/coach

Rob is also looking for more participants for future vol-umes of *Attraction Marketing and Networking Professionals*. Please drop him a line if you know of someone you think he should interview!

Learn more at:
http://attractionmarketing.50interviews.com

ABOUT 50 INTERVIEWS

Imagine a university where each student not only gets a textbook custom tailored to curriculum they personally designed, but where each student literally becomes the author!

The mission of 50 Interviews, Inc. is to provide aspiring, passionate, driven people a framework to achieve their dreams of becoming that which they aspire to be. Learning what it takes to be the best in your field directly from those who have already succeeded. The ideal author is someone who desires to be a recognized expert in their field. You will be part of a community of authors who share your passion and who have learned firsthand how the 50 Interviews concept works. A form of extreme education, the process will transform you into that which you aspire to become.

Looking to dramatically alter the course of your life? First go have some conversations with those who do what you think you might like to emulate. Find out what drives them and how they found success. Then rewrite your future, one interview at a time...

50 Interviews is a career change process where you first fully explore potential future careers. BEFORE making any risky commitments, you first spend time talking to those who do the job you think you would love to try next, with top professionals in their field! While gaining from their experience and knowledge, YOU gain great mentoring tips, phenomenal connections, and then share those with others in your own 50 Interviews title as the author of your own book!

50 Interviews is a showcase of people living their dreams,

and enjoying the payoff that results from taking the leap to explore something they are truly passionate about! Learn the truth about the challenges and the rewards of whatever field interests you. Gain valuable advice from people who were once in your shoes. If you don't make a change now, will you ever? Sure you have doubts, but how else will you learn everything about pursuing that dream job? Your interviews will shed light on what has inspired and driven others to follow their dreams and how those dreams have manifested for them. It is a way to collect over 50 new mentors who might inspire you and prove that anything is possible, and then you can share that knowledge with the world through your own publication.

Each 50 Interviews book title is determined by the author who chooses the career they would like to explore in depth. By interviewing top professionals in that field, you gain a glimpse into the vital mindset of those successful in your field of choice, and then use that knowledge to take you one step closer to their own definition of success. If you are interested in learning more, I would love to hear from you! You can contact me via email at: brian@50interviews. com, by phone: 970-215-1078 (Colorado), or through our website: www.50interviews.com.

Reinvent yourself – one interview at a time,

Brian Schwartz
Authorpreneur and Creator of 50 Interviews

More 50 Interviews Titles

Additional topics based on the 50 Interviews model that have already been released or are in development:

50 Athletes over 50
By Don McGrath

Video Marketing Pioneers
By Randy Berry

Young Entrepreneurs
By Nick Tart and Nick Scheidies

Professional Speakers
By Laura Lee Carter & Brian Schwartz

Artists
By Maryann Swartz

Franchisees
By Leslie Lautzenhiser

Spiritualists
By Tuula Fai

Actors
By Stella Hannah

Physicians in Transition
By Rich Fernadnez, MD

Wealth Managers
By Allen Duck

Direct Selling Millionaires
By Kirsten McCay-Smith

Entrepreneurs
By Brian Schwartz

Property Managers
By Michael Levy

Visit **www.50interviews.com** for a complete and current list.

www.ingramcontent.com/pod-product-compliance
Lightning Source LLC
Chambersburg PA
CBHW031122020426
42333CB00012B/191